A Christian Mother's Survival Guide

Making a Living
while Raising your
Family at Home

Iris Shamble

Copyright 2005 by Iris Shamble

All Scripture references are from the New King James Version of the Bible unless otherwise noted.

All rights reserved. No part of this book may be reproduced or transmitted in any form or by any means, electronic or mechanical, including photocopying, recording or by any information storage and retrieval system, without permission in writing from Faith Unlimited, 7305 Middleton Drive, Fredericksburg, VA 22407.

Second Edition July 2005
ISBN: 1-933265-48-5
Printed in the United States of America

Author & Publisher: Iris Shamble
Cover Design: Charlene Davis
Editor: Elizabeth Latrobe Place
Web Design & Layout: Marsh Durham

www.achristianmothersguide.com

Table of Contents

Preface — 1

Chapter 1
A Woman of Worth — 3

Chapter 2
Understanding Your Spouse — 19

Chapter 3
Children – A Heritage from the Lord — 28

Chapter 4
Achieving Victory as a Single Mother — 46

Chapter 5
The Complete Homemaker — 53

Chapter 6
Telecommuting, Telework and Hottest Scams — 64

Chapter 7
Great Legitimate Work at Home
& Home schooling Resources — 72

Chapter 8
The Daily Word — 88

Preface

My message for all women is to let you know that your responsibility as a wife and mother should never be compromised. I want to share encouragement and Scripture to help you through many problems you may face in life. Single or married, you should feel blessed, whether you are a working woman outside of your home, or a woman in your home mothering full-time. I believe you will find in this book, many answers to questions and thoughts that you have had.

As a woman, we create the atmosphere in our homes. If momma ain't happy, nobody is happy...right?

As a mother, do you question your priorities? What comes first? Is it your husband, your children, your friends, your job, your home, your faith? It should not be a quandary as all are equally important and all are intertwined. Faith supports my many roles as does my husband. As a wife I feel love, protection, and most of all security from my husband. As a wife and mother, we have to assure our spouse, he is well deserving of the responsibility God has given him. It should not be a competition, but an honor.

Proverbs 18:22 "He who finds a wife finds what is good, and obtains favor from the Lord."

We have made a commitment to our husband and our families. How we honor and serve them is a great challenge. One of the greatest challenges today is finding the means to maintain a constant presence in our homes.

***Psalms 128:3** "Your wife shall be like a fruitful vine, in the very heart of her house."*

Ask yourself if you are the heart of your home? It can be a goal for all of us. I am not advocating that women leave their jobs. We have to use wisdom in every decision we make for our family, and only you know what is right for yours. I only suggest that you pray, examine your own life and come to know who you are so that you can move in greater strength as a godly woman in your home. Take inventory of yourself; look closely to see what you can change and then ask God to help you. We all learn lessons in different ways; for some it is more difficult than others, but the important point is -- we have learned a lesson.

Chapter One

A Woman of Worth!

I must begin by saying a woman of worth is a virtuous woman;

Who can find a virtuous wife? For her worth is far above rubies. The heart of her husband safely trusts her; so he will have no lack of gain. She does him good and not evil, all the days of her life. Proverbs 31: 10-12

We must have many attributes that make us stand out as godly women. As women we must be of great strength to uphold our household. We should raise up our family's social position and be an example to younger women.

The older women likewise, that they be reverent in behavior, not slanderers, not given to much wine, teachers of good things, that they admonish the young women to love their husbands, to love their children, to be discreet, chaste and most of all homemakers, good, obedient to their own husbands, that the word of God may not be blasphemed. Titus 2: 3-5

When a mother dreams, she has visions of raising children that will be loving, respectable, honest, compassionate and most of all successful in life. It takes work, it takes prayer, and most of all it takes faith. Faith is simply taking God at his word. Trusting God totally.

Hebrews 11:1 Now Faith is the substance of things hoped for, the evidence of things not seen.

I talk with many younger ladies and I share the importance of being a godly woman. I let them know they don't have to compromise their lifestyles to be a woman in their home. The world's view is always changing whether it is about clothing, family, lifestyles; but God's word is always the same.

Hebrews 13:8 Jesus Christ is the same yesterday, today and forever.

My mother showed love to me as I was growing up and raised me with what she knew as a single mother. She made great sacrifices, and I am thankful for it. I believe it truly paid off in my life. I must say however, had she known the Lord in her earlier years many things would have worked out differently. But hey, at least we got started.

This is why it is imperative for those of us, who are rooted and grounded in the Word of God, to share and be an example to younger woman and those in need. A woman's day is not long enough to show everything we do. Later in this book, I will share with you results of statistics regarding the amount of money it would take to replace a mother and all the roles she fills.

A woman's worth is far more than the worth of rubies. When God created us, we were given an important role to fulfill and with his guidance we can accomplish it with great strength. We have to see ourselves as rubies, as valuable human beings! As wives we are to be respectful to our husbands, support them, and encourage them to be who God called them to be.

I am not talking to women that have the spirit of Jezebel; a spirit that hates men, and wants to destroy the headship. I am not talking to women that do not believe in God.

Psalm 14:1 the fool has said in his heart, there is no God".

Genesis 1:7 "And the Lord God formed man of the dust of the ground, and breathed into his nostrils".

I am talking to women who understand and are confident about their role in their homes as wives and mothers. I am talking to women who attempt to bring joy to every situation in the home. Is any day without trials? No, but it is still a blessed day. Trials can truly strengthen us when we least expect it. It is like this. When you go to school and you pass and complete one grade, you go to the next and so on. It is no different in our faith-filled lives. Our daily walk with God is as a test, and how we handle it and pass each test is what qualifies us for the big exam. Tests may be such things as impatience, lack of love and forgiveness. When we walk out these challenges by applying the Word of God, we can easily see ourselves completing and passing life's many tests. Before you know it, what once bothered you before has no effect on you. That is what I am talking about in passing the big exam. This can be looked at as personal development. We can grow physically, but we must also pay attention to our spiritual development.

If you are not sure of your role as a wife and mother, you've come to the right place. By the time I deliver my message to you, I believe you will be enlightened and be ready to make great changes in your life.

I encourage myself daily and that is what we have to do because no one will do it for us. We must make and take time and spend it in the Word. Spending time early in the day with God will make a difference in your life. We all know the old saying "the early bird gets the worm". This is also true when spending time with God first thing in the morning. You will get a handle on your day and anything the enemy has planned for you will have no power to prosper.

Isaiah 54:17 No weapon formed against you shall prosper, and every tongue which rises against you in judgment you shall condemn.

There may be days when you need a little more encouragement, but the important thing is to keep God's word as final authority.

I am also talking to women who are not easily offended by what others say, and are not afraid of the word "submit". Most women have been taught the word submit is a dirty word. Not according to the Bible.

Ephesians 5:22 Wives, submit to your husbands, as to the Lord.

Now ask yourself, are you committed to the Lord? If not, you may rethink that at the end of my message. We must not worry about what our husbands are doing or not doing, but focus on being committed to the Lord and pray for our husbands and God will honor our prayers.

We have to seek God and ask for wisdom in any circumstance that comes into our life.

Proverbs 14:1 says "The wise woman builds her house, But the foolish pulls it down with her hands".

There is nothing too difficult for God.

Genesis 18:14 is there anything to hard for the Lord?

As women we must build our home up, not tear it down. As wives and mothers we have been specially equipped. We have been equipped to be doctors, lawyers, teachers, advisors, taxis, lovers. This list can go on and on. We are not defined by what society says we are, but as God defines us.

Proverbs 31:30 Favour is deceitful, and beauty is vain, but a woman that feareth the Lord, she shall be praised.

Our husbands and children look good, because we look good. God's Word shares with us the order for the home. God knows how the family should be. He created it!

A lot of us have not been prepared to be wives and mothers. We have dreams of being a great wife and mother. We don't just have to wonder, we can have our dreams and hopes of making a blessed home come true. As children we didn't know what true joy was until we came into the real knowledge of the Word of God. Daily, it is still a learning experience. Each day we should expect and know that God has something good in that day for us. Each year we should make progress in our life as well. Always remember Christ came, so that we would have life and have it more abundantly.

3 John 1:2, Beloved, I pray that you may prosper in all things and be in health, even as your soul prospers.

We were not prepared for the roles of being a wife, mother, friend, lawyer, doctor, lover, advisor, but they are all within us. These attributes have to be developed, nurtured, and caressed in a way that they become exposed. When this happens we have no problems submitting to our spouses. When we are confident in ourselves, the plan and purpose of our family will be in order. Did you know submission means that you are coming under the mission of another? To actively submit, actually causes us to be protected and covered. Who in their right mind wants to be in this world without any covering or protection from God?

As mothers, we are here to train our children to be godly children. We are here to be an example to them. We have to teach our children about authority, and what it means to submit properly. One thing for sure, we must be their friends. Make sure you keep a balance as a mother. A friend is one that is "attached to another by affection", "is a favored companion", "one who shows kindly interest and goodwill." Now if that is not an attribute of a mother, and a wife, I just don't know what is!

If you are a woman that has not committed your life to Christ, I again plead with you; make that personal decision today because, if you are not submitted to God, then there is no way you can honestly submit to your husband. Whenever there is a disruption in fellowship between a husband and wife, there is more than likely a break in fellowship with the Lord Jesus Christ.

We must continue to prepare our home for an atmosphere of love through continued prayer. When the man is not walking in his full potential in the home, we must help cultivate and help him to be what God has called him to be. After all, our spouses should be as a pastor and teacher in the home. As women, we surely can help shape our husbands. I know it seems odd, but a woman or wife can make or break her man. In a family there should be no shame from anyone. This is a family commitment, and we should walk in this relationship as one. Neither is more important than the other. We balance each other. What you may be good at, your spouse may not be and vice versa, that is why we balance each other. A husband and wife functioning openly and freely in their relationship, provide a solid foundation on which joy, peace and love can easily operate in a Christian home. One vital thing to remember is that it doesn't happen overnight. It takes faith to please God, and likewise, we have to walk out situations in our life by faith. Some people tend to make things mysterious when you talk about walking by faith. When we actually walk by faith everyday, we will succeed, even unbelievers. It is like when we go to work and expect pay after a 40 hour work week. We don't know if the company we worked for will or has gone into bankruptcy. We believe we are going to get paid. We also expect our family members to return home each day after we go our separate ways. When we go to start our car, we are simply expecting it to start. This is all by faith.

Hebrews 11:6 But without faith it is impossible to please God.

Please remember your faith will never rise above the level of knowledge that you have in any area. That is why is it crucial to study to Word of God on a regularly basis.

Whether it is a time in your life where different areas erupt in your home such as: strife, rebellion, discord, you must speak to that situation by applying the word of God and walk it out. At times, your faith in God may be challenged because things are getting worse instead of better. That is almost a sure sign that a blessing is just about to take place in your life. The truth is a lot of people cave in and quit before they see victory in their situation. They give up much too soon. I have often shared with many women that persistence is one of the keys to success in life. It's not always easy, but it is achievable. You must keep at it and faith will help you do that.

At one time in my marriage, I tended to be a bit prideful. I learned that is no way to be. I believe that my pride cost us an unnecessary financial burden. The answers and directions were right inside my husband, but I was too prideful to ask for help. We must let our spouses know what we are thinking. Believe me, they cannot read our minds.

I have had people tell me they can feel the peace in our home. I tell you this; it took prayer and action behind the prayer. To this day, it still takes prayer! I pray daily to maintain peace in our home. Satan tries to raise his ugly head, but as soon as I recognize any tactic of the devil, I speak to it and let the devil know he has no place in my life.

Luke 10:19 Behold, I give you power to tread on serpents and scorpions, and over all the power of the enemy: and nothing shall by any means hurt you.

Do I always feel I have conquered evil at that time? No, I don't, but I don't cave in and quit. I continue to speak the Word of God and face my situation. The Word clearly says we have what we say.

Proverbs 18:21 Death and life and in the power of the tongue: and they that love it shall eat the fruit thereof.

If we want to change how things are going in our lives, we have to speak them. The authority is right in us. Whatever the reasons that you believe God, you must speak those reasons into existence. After all, God spoke this world into existence. We become what we visualize ourselves to be. The same applies to what we say. If we speak negatively, we are going to receive negativity. If you see yourself as having low self-esteem, depressed, frustrated – guess what? You are going to have low self-esteem, be depressed and frustrated. But if on the contrary, you see yourself as a mighty woman of God, a woman of character, a thinker, full of wit and love, and most of all full of faith, you will be what you visualize and what you say! Things can easily come upon us if we allow them to get the best of us. Walk smarter than the enemy.

When a mother is forced to work out of the home, most men still expect her to keep the house up, cook, clean, care for the children and perform her best sexually. Come on now…let's be real. Actually we are responsible for maintaining two jobs. As women again, we must continue to pray, seek God's word to strengthen us and do our best as the woman of our house. Our husbands are willing to give us what we want, but we must not step out of our Godly roles and challenge them. Believe it or not, we don't have to manipulate our husbands; we just have to show love and joy.

If you are a woman working outside your home and desire to be in your home, just continue to be the wife that God called you to be. Even on your job, let your Christ-like ways be recognized in the workplace. We are a living epistle. A letter read by all men. Walk in integrity; always do what is right even when no one is looking. I tell my children this often. They will even say, "Well everybody does it". And I kindly say to them – "you're not"! I tell them that they will be accountable for their actions and stand before the Lord one day. You don't want to shorten your blessings and days on earth over something so simple.

As a woman of worth, I hold on to my commitment of taking care of the inside of the home. Now, our kids play a good part in our home as well. What a relief! They do work for their monthly allowances. I want them to be involved enough to know, they do have to work for the things in life they desire

If you feel Satan at your door, don't sign for the package, be smarter than he is and find a way to fend him off with the Word of God. Whether you make a decision to pray, read or just relax, make it a quality decision. I know as women, we tend to always have something to do or at least find something to do. It is important to just take time out, sit down and ask God to refresh you; restore you; strengthen you. While you sit there just close your eyes and meditate on the goodness of God, and feel his presence come in.

The enemy is defeated, but that doesn't stop him from trying to bring hate and discontent into the home. Have you ever wondered why he tries to attack when things are at their best? He comes because you are just about at one of the best blessings God has for you at that time, and his job is to distract and discourage you. Don't fall into his trap.

When you have made a commitment to share your life together, you have to remember commitment takes work. It has trials, but the reward for enduring them is great! That is marriage –not mirage. Take time right here just to jot down the good things you see and adore in your spouse. We are not even looking at the bad. We are focusing on the good. Focusing on the good is what brings greatness into our lives.

Just to let you in on a little secret, I'm not perfect! I know my husband loves me. One thing you can count on with your husband,--if he takes good care of his mother, he will take good care of you. My husband shows love and concern for his mother and it rolled right down to me. His mother gave herself and supported him strongly, and I know this had a great influence on him as a man and husband.

We all have areas we need to work on daily. We have to have our minds renewed. Renew means getting rid of the old and replacing it with new. Change isn't change, until something has changed! We can't expect things to be different if we still speak the same way or act the same way. We should never just settle with unpleasing ways and say, "that's just the way I am." That could be detrimental to your marriage and to your life. I had to make a decision to keep the Word of God a priority in my life; continually praying and letting God handle every situation. I definitely keep doing my part as a faithful wife, loving my husband. Things that I don't agree with or like, I keep in prayer. One thing we must remember, our thoughts determine our destiny. To avoid conflict, I either talk to my husband about it, or send him an email in love. Hey, you have to do what you have to do to get the attention needed in your home. People react in different ways to different things, and I learned my husband was much more receptive when I send him a lovely email with questions, concerns and of course an encouraging word to top it all off – like "we got a date tonight"? Talk about getting his attention. I am not ashamed to say this works for us. We found what works for us but for you it might be a letter, nice dinner, a romantic night together. A lot of times the change has to start with us. The wife who truly loves her husband will make his happiness her primary goal. With this kind of motivation you'll both be winners. Never think he wins by getting his way. Look at it like a reward that will make life better for you and him. After all -- you married him! Whatever you want to reap, that is what you need to sow! You want peace--sow peace. You want more love--then sow more love.

As I grew in the ways of God, I learned to focus more on my husband and things did change. I encouraged our girls to support their dad more. I realized I had to involve them as well, so they would know what is important in a marriage. I think a lot of people miss this when they are not willing to change or give up something they enjoy or don't enjoy. Sounds strange, but we can get so religious that whatever we do becomes such a ritual. It does not affect our lives. If we allow that to happen, we are looking for failure. Some people want to stick to the same way mama and daddy did it, regardless of the frustration that existed in that home. I want our daughters to see the importance of supporting a godly man in the home. I often try to show more interest in things he is interested in and encourage them to do so. Do I know anything about golf, basketball, and softball? No way! If he enjoys these things, I try my best to enjoy them too. I also surround myself with men and women of God, people I know I can trust, and I learn from them. I continually build friendships with men and women of God that I know are anchored in the Word, and I build from their friendships. I enjoy friendships that will help me enhance my life and marriage. You can't continue to be with people who are constantly having problems. You can't grow or gain anything from listening to your friend complain about her spouse. After awhile, it may even weaken your thoughts and pattern of thinking.

I thank God for the anointed leaders God has placed in the life of my husband and me. They are truly leaders we know we can call on. These are leaders that truly emulate how we as children of God are supposed to be. One's compassionate about teaching the Word of God. Being under anointed leaders that truly follow God will enhance your growth and development in the Lord and your marriage.

Ephesians 4:11-12 And he gave some apostles; and some, prophets; and some, evangelists; and some, pastors and teachers; For the perfecting of the saints, for the work of the ministry, for the edifying of the body of Christ.

It is imperative for you to join a local church. That is where your strength and development will come from. The teachings our pastor's share with us is so vital in our everyday life. How can you measure what they do for us? Not only should our pastors teach with boldness and authority, their life should be an example before us.

One of the most important things that a woman must realize is that her husband will have to stand before God for the deeds good or bad he did for his family, and give an account of them. What I hope this message does is encourage wives and mothers to make whatever changes they must to have homes that God would be pleased with. I wish for you a home that is filled with joy and peace all the time. Yes, there will always be challenges, but we can overcome them all and not be overtaken. Will we make mistakes? We surely will, but God is still there for us.

As a wife and mother we bring healing to all situations. I guess you could say we have a gift of healing. That's just the way it is. Our role as mothers is crucial to raising children that will grow up as godly children respecting and serving the Lord. Our role as wives is to prepare the atmosphere in our homes.

Psalm 128: 3 your wife shall be like a fruitful vine, in the very heart of your house, your children like olive plants all around your table.

A fruitful vine produces good fruit. As a wife and mother we should represent good fruit; Love--builds them all.

Galatians 5:22 love, joy, peace, long-suffering, kindness, goodness, faithfulness.

One thing that is important is we should never shut our children out, they should always feel they can come and talk to us. We should always have an open door. If we don't, believe me, Satan will open his door, and yes he will listen to them. Now let me share this with you, if you are not producing these fruits, it is not a time to condemn yourself, it is a time to pray, seek God's face, and stay in the Word of God.

We all face different challenges at different times of our lives. This does not make us bad parents if we are dealing with issues that others are not. Remember there is always someone, somewhere that would happily exchange places with you.

If we want to walk as children of God, we must always learn God's way of doing things. We must not settle for less, we must not accept any offer or opportunity the world gives us. We must not compromise! Each and every day as I pray, I thank God for another great day, and I expect good and favor in that day. Favor simply indicates that you are treated gently and with kindness, and have great advantages, and have much support. I also declare my life is redeemed from destruction! This means I am protected from any harm or danger when you walk with the Lord.

Psalm 103:4 who redeems your life from destruction.

It is a MUST! The enemy will not only try to come into our lives for what we don't know, but mostly for what we have been taught. You must know how to apply the Word for every situation. Another good thing about being in favor is that people around you often benefit as well. I tell you as I started confessing and looking forward to good things and favor everyday, more and more favor came everyday whether I was in line at the grocery store or gas station, people went out of their way for me. If it was just to give me the first place in a line, I gave thanks for it.

When you keep yourself girded in the Word of God and in prayer, you will see more victories in your life. Most people are in a state of reactionary faith. That is they react to the situation then try to deal with it. One thing about reactionary faith you can lose ground fast. The reason is you will have nothing built in you to help you survive when you most need it. One man of God described it as an emergency room. People come in with emergency situations, some make it, and some don't. They depend on nurses and doctors to help them overcome their problem. On the other hand there is pro-active faith. This is faith that helps you prepare for any situation that comes upon you. You have confessed the Word of God daily, made your confession about your life and you are ready for anything. Instead of having a good marriage-- you set the stage for a great marriage. Instead of getting over an episode of bad health--you walk in divine healing. One last thing, instead of overcoming a bad financial situation--you are financially free, because you never get in financial bondage. Testimonies are great as a result of people overcoming situations, but to never be in that situation and keep your faith pro-active is greater!

I feel what God placed in my heart he wants me to share with women. It rubs me the wrong way when I hear people say it takes two working people to make it as a family. Look at the picture honestly. God placed man and woman here on this earth to bring forth children. If both husband and wife work, this limits their time with their children. Daycare, school, community activities take their place, then I have to ask," What is the purpose of the mother and father?"

As we walk before God, he will give us instructions and guidance to be the best wife and mother we can be.

Psalm 119:10-11 "With my whole heart I have sought you; oh, let me not wander from your commandments! Your word I have hidden in my heart that I might not sin against you."

There are a lot of things our parents did which perhaps were wrong. The simple fact is they were doing the best they could, with what they knew. I tell you this; there is no better way, than doing it God's way. I converse with my husband more about the need for both of us to work outside the home. Because men are goal oriented, they don't see results as we see them. What they see is RIGHT NOW! They see a goal. It's harder for a man to totally rely on God, but I tell you, once he totally submits to God, aint no devil in hell gonna stop him. I don't believe men would deliberately want to take away from their children; they just look at what they want for the family later in the future.

All this is good, but at the expense of our time with our children. It is obvious men and women are different-- not only physically, but mentally. As women, our feelings come straight from the heart, whereas men's feelings come straight from the head. Thus they have to be cultivated a little bit. I do not make light of this, because this next statement is true. It is said men only use half of their brain. What they do with the other half, I have no idea. While we women use all our brain, plus theirs. We talk more, share more, and give more. Is anything wrong with that? No, we just have to accept our husbands as they are.

Right now statistics show that the average man spends about 45 seconds a day with their children under the age of 3. How sad is that?

Now if you are a wife and mother with an unsaved spouse, love your husband to Christ. Many men have been turned to the Lord because of their wife's conduct.

1 Peter 3:3-4 Do not let your adornment be merely outward – arranging the hair, wearing gold, or putting on fine apparel – rather let it be the hidden person of the heart, with the incorruptible beauty of a gentle and quiet spirit, which is very precious in the sight of God.

We have to accept our husbands for who they are. It does take time and patience, but through Christ we can do all things. Surround your husband with prayer and understanding. Also the wife needs the filling of the Holy Spirit to remain steady and calm. Your husband truly needs you to understand him. Don't compete with him or nag him, but try to help him and most of all please him. Show respect to him at all times! I know I have been guilty of not showing respect many times. I wanted my husband to be in his rightful place as the head of the household and instead of constantly speaking to that situation, I would approach it in the wrong way. That didn't help, so what I decided to do is find a scripture that I could apply to my situation and confess and believe for victory. If you feel you need such a scripture and confession to help you, please take time to speak this prayer over your spouse.

Ephesians 3: 16-19
That he would grant (spouse name), according to the riches of His glory, to be strengthened with might through His Spirit in the inner man. That Christ may dwell in (spouse name) heart through faith; that (spouse name) , being rooted and grounded in love, may be able to comprehend with all the saints what is the width and length and depth and height – to know the love of Christ which passes knowledge; that (Spouse name) may be filled with all the fullness of God.

If you are involved with a local church, don't be so involved as to take you away from your husband's needs. He will resent this. It may cause him to stay away from the church longer. I remember my husband saying to me several years ago; you don't nag like you use to. That encouraged me to know I had grown a great deal, and I was very proud of myself. Do I mess up sometimes? Yes, I surely do, but I don't condemn myself, I speak into my own situation. Life and death is in the power of our tongues. We either speak well into our life or bad. Was it easy to shut my mouth? Not all the time, but it is a continual growing process. To this day, I still have to bite my lip. I share this message to bless your home, because I realize how important it is to have a home that God would be pleased with.

God will hold us accountable for our actions, as well as what we allow our family members to do. We have to make the decision to change. Like a lot of marriages, Darryl and I were out in the world together. Then I made the obvious decision to serve the Lord, and in his time, he did also.

Make sure as a wife, you don't share your husband's downfalls with others, especially within your family. You don't want one end being pulled by prayer, and the other by strife. Family and friends often remember and hold on to the negative things we tell them. Avoid that downfall from day one.

I tell you this, a lot of the time our little paycheck is not the problem, it is our lack of wisdom and understanding for not being a proper steward over that paycheck. I did without buying outfits, shoes, and other things for myself for awhile because I wanted to sacrifice for our goals as a family. I worked outside of the home while preparing this book, because I didn't want to take away from our established budget. It was a sacrifice I was willing to make to get this message out. I desire to be back in my home, and I know as I prepare this book, it's just a matter of time before I will be again. Many of the websites and businesses I will share with you have helped me attain jobs working in my home. If you are serious about staying at home, don't give up! You have a destiny to fulfill. Being persistent and with prayer you can achieve it.

We are achieving happiness by applying the Word of God to our lives, living it daily and confessing the Word constantly. I really want to stress how important it is to know we have what we say. Even if your belief in God is being challenged, don't be discouraged, keep applying faith and making your confessions.

Because men are so goal orientated, we often have a problem getting our husbands to understand, we might say, "baby if you could just romance me up a little while before lovemaking begins, it would go a lot smoother!" All they see is the target and boy do they go for it? Again, that not a bad thing, it is just how it is approached. The authority they carry within them is hard to cover up. One woman of God I had the opportunity to be under once shared with the ladies - there is two times to have sex--when you feel like it and when you don't. I told her – "Pastor, by faith I will get there."

I tell you it is something to keep up with our husbands, but enjoying sex with your spouse is an important aspect of marriage. Husbands desire great sexual fulfillment and wives must be there to accommodate their needs. If we are not there to fulfill their needs, there is someone who will try to fill our shoes. We can not let that happen.

Another great woman of God told the women of one church that if we could have sex for seven straight days, we would see a breakthrough in our marriages. Whew! I know seven is the number of completion, and eight represents new beginnings. Sex can also create new beginnings for our marriages. Spice it up; date your husband all over again!

I love my husband very much, and I love how he can accomplish certain tasks in the home. However, as a woman there are certain things that we are most tuned in to, and we must stand strong and pray and see those things come to pass. There is absolutely nothing wrong with that. It may take time for us to see things as our husbands do, but in time we will! We have all looked at things as they are in the natural world. We have to also see them in the spiritual.

Romans 4:17 as it is written, "I have made you a father of many nations" in the presence of Him whom he believed God, who gives life to the dead and calls those things which do not exist as though they did.

As believers we walk in the spiritual not in the natural. Everything that exists originated in the spiritual realm. That is why I walk by faith, not by sight.

2 Cor 5:7 for we walk by faith, not by sight.

Chapter Two

Understanding Your Spouse

He is a provider, protector, comforter, leader, lover and a warrior. God gave him his first assignment right in the Garden of Eden.

Genesis 2:15 Then the Lord God took the man and put him in the Garden of Eden to tend and keep it. Genesis 2:18 And the Lord God said: "it is not good that man should be alone; I will make him a helper comparable to him."

God did not go to Eve in the garden; God went straight to Adam. Even in your family you go to the person with authority when a situation arises. So God put the man in the leadership position. Now, does that mean because man is in a leadership position, he has everything under control? Absolutely not! God gave him a helper, someone comparable to him. God gave man someone who was adaptable to him, someone to enhance him. God gave him a woman. So though the old saying says dog is man's best friend, we know better! The Bible states that God took one of Adam's ribs and made woman.

Genesis 2: 21 - 22, And the Lord caused a deep sleep to fall on Adam, and he slept; and He took one of his ribs, and closed up the flesh in its place. Then the rib, which the Lord God had taken from man, He made into a woman, and He brought her to the man.

Now when something is taken away from one thing, it clearly means that part, is incomplete. It is no different than a puzzle. If one piece is missing, that puzzle is incomplete. So, now man is complete-- with woman. We are a team!

Let me back up for a moment and throw this in for free-- according to God's word, there is no such thing as what our society now refers to as – 'a significant other'. God made male and female to create a family. Common sense tells us if you are not able to produce another human being together, it is not the design of God.

Leviticus 20:13 If a man lies with a male as he lies with a woman, both of them shall surely be put to death.

Same principles apply for the woman.
The man also has the responsibility of submitting to his wife.

Ephesians 5:25 Husbands, love your wives, just as Christ also loved the church and gave Himself for her.

There must not be anything separating the husband and the Lord. When someone gives his or her life for you that is a serious covenant. It is a covenant that should not be broken. We seem to have a problem with submitting to our husbands, yet we go outside to the working secular world, and submit to our unsaved bosses with no problems. Before marriage, during my foolish days when I was unsaved, I use to say things like – I ain't obeying any man, because I am the lady. I felt the man better be happy with me or just miss out. Boy was I wrong! A husband is one that conquers and protects us. Part of man's responsibility is to fight for his home spiritually. He is to be a warrior, to stand head to head with any demonic force that tries to go against his family. I know there are a lot of men that are not in their proper roles in the home. I know families where the man stays home while the wife goes to church. Boy is that backwards. How can he love his family as Christ loved the church, if he does not learn how to? But as women, we must continually stay in the face of God, not in our man's face. I have been guilty of that. One important thing I have learned is to go to God, not my spouse. That just causes friction and more tension. It can also raise the spirit of rebellion. You do not want your spouse to shut the door to God in his life. Be very careful of this!

Your efforts will not go unnoticed by God or your husband. If you fulfill your role and respect your husband, I believe this allows a willing spirit to come upon your husband. As a woman, I love sharing what my husband has done for me. What woman wouldn't want to brag on her husband and show how well he is taking care of her? It is great to have a nice home, drive a nice car and know that your husband provide for you.

My husband faithfully takes care of our yard, cars and home. True, his drive and spirit sometimes make me want to say SIT DOWN! He always has to have something to do. I like to get the job done, but I also like to sit, relax and enjoy time doing plain old nothing! My husband and I made a commitment to maintain our home and he keeps his word. I don't think I could have it any better.

As women when we put more into understanding our spouse, we begin to see things in a different light. When a man decides to marry a woman, he should come to her fully prepared to take care of her financially. The problem is in most marriages these days is that we bring too much debt into our marriages. Then the wife is forced to go outside the home to work. I say, if a newly married couple were to base their living solely on the salary of the husband, a wife could be in her home and be comfortable when they decide to have children. But what happens? We want the new cars, new furniture, everything new and we get strapped with too much debt. Even when the wife works before having children, if her salary were properly budgeted, when they have children she would be easily available for them in the home. I wish I had understood this when I married. I could have saved a lot of unwanted credit card bills, and our children could have enjoyed a lot more things during certain times. Not that they lacked anything, but there were times when we could not give them the things they wanted. The reason, the money had to go to a creditor. That aint GOD! Thank God that we have been blessed over the years and are able to do a lot more than in the earlier years in our marriage.

God gave man this great responsibility, and we should by no means take advantage of it. However, when a man fails to follow God's plan and purpose for his life, this causes a woman to have to go outside the home to work, and causes the family to be unbalanced. One thing is for sure, once you totally depend on God, you will never want for anything. There will always be a door of opportunity waiting for you. Sometimes we walk through the wrong door, but it is up to us to back up and go through the right door.

When the Bible speaks of the <u>wife</u> being submissive to her husband;

Ephesians 5:22 Wives, submit to your own husbands, as to the Lord.

When you are under submission to someone, that means they protect you, and you assist them. It should also mean they have a plan for life, and the family's life. The problem is that a lot of men are out of place in the home and therefore cause the woman to take a leadership role spiritually and that gives her a lot of unnecessary burden and responsibility that God never intended the woman to have.

The Bible also clearly states:

Ephesians 5:25 Husbands love your wives just as Christ loved the Church and gave himself for her.

When our husbands really know God, and have an intimate relationship with him, there will be no basketball game, no fishing trip, and no golf game that comes before his family. Let me make myself clear-- there is nothing wrong with any of these things, it is just a matter of setting priorities. There were many times that I felt frustrated when my husband put softball, baseball, and golf before our family. One thing I came to realize is that I have to be accountable for what I feel and do, and my husband has to as well. One thing I also came to realize was, the way he spent time was not the same way that I spent time with God. Therefore, I had to learn to hush my mouth.

I tell you this; I know it is hard when your husband continually looks for the remote control over you, when he lies on the sofa like there is no tomorrow. I know what you are talking about! I have been there, done that!

What I did was take a closer look at how my husband provides for his family and all that he does for us, and the good definitely out-weighs the not so good. In understanding our spouse, we have to find good in everything, because if we don't the negative will consume us and pretty soon we will either be having a pity party or be consumed with anger.

Prayer is what changes things. Today my husband is careful when making his plans. He tries to avoid conflicts that will take him away from the house of the Lord and his family.

We must also renew our minds. The mind is where the battle takes place. It actually controls our destiny. We are products of our thoughts and actions we have walked out. I always keep in mind how well my husband provides for our family. He makes sure we have what we need and he takes care of the home quickly whenever anything needs attention. If something is not working properly, believe me he fixes it right away. When I look at the interest he has in sports and outside activities and how he balances it with how he provides for his family, I feel gratitude and thankfulness for the husband God gave me. Now there are certainly places for improvement on both our parts. A lot of times, I don't see it in the natural, but I do believe it in the spirit. I try to focus on what I can do to make things better. One thing I have learned, and it took me awhile to do so, was definitely not to confront my husband while he was holding that remote control. Talk about a loaded weapon! I often tease my husband, and tell him "step away from the remote". As women, we like to talk and sometimes not at the most opportune times. I have come to the conclusion; we cannot compete with ESPN. Sometimes I still make mistakes and I want to talk during the big game, but I am learning. I do try to wait until my husband has enjoyed his sports, before I ask any serious questions. That's just the way it is! Why start a conflict when there doesn't have to be one?

God created Adam first, and gave him a job.

Genesis 2:15 Then God took the man and put him in the Garden of Eden to tend and keep it.

God gave the man the responsibility for providing for his family. God didn't create the woman to fight temptation and struggle with evil. What man in his right mind would want to force his wife out amongst such forces? When the husband and father is not in his proper role, that means the family is also not in the role God intended them to be in. There are a lot of women who are the disciplinarians in their homes. That is not the way it should be. I was in that position once. I used to issue a lot of the disciplinary actions in our home and I tell you it was no fun. I will also let you know there were times if I had kept my mouth closed things would have worked out differently. As I have allowed my husband to be more involved in decisions that are made about our children, I have seen great changes. I told him it is never too late to work on making changes. Men may not share their feelings as we do, but I have found that that does not mean they don't care. They do care; they just express it in a different way. One man of God shared with us this thought – that we live in a two-story house, his story and my story. I thought that was cute.

I could have chosen to focus on what we haven't accomplished, but I made the choice to forget the past. I said to myself, just look at God. The entire household from the head down should be serving the Lord. The husband and father should not only be an example to his wife, but also to his children. How he treats his wife should show his children what to look for in a spouse. He should set an example to his sons, as to how to treat a woman and wife. He should set examples to his daughters as to what to expect from a man and husband. The father shouldn't be shy or uneasy. He should tell his daughters and sons that he loves them. Don't sell men short, one thing about men is they may not seem to be paying attention to things being said or going on around them, but they soak it in. They always surprise me!

When a man is in his proper role in the home, as first of all a man of God, it is no problem for a wife to follow his leadership. When you see your husband truly worshipping and fellowshipping with God, you will give your all to make sure his every need is met. He would never have a sexless night! Right? But when he is not in his proper role, it is hard not to act like a complete nut around him. But I will say this, even if your spouse is not walking in total submission to God, you must continue to walk with God and let your lifestyle be seen.

1 Tim 2: 9-10 in like manner also, that the women adorn themselves in modest apparel, with propriety and moderation, not with braided hair or gold or pearls or costly clothing, but, which is proper for women profession Godliness, with good works.

Let your spouse see you changing and pretty soon, I believe, he also will want to know the Jesus you serve. There was a time when I was going to church regularly but my husband wasn't. Pretty soon, he wanted to come to visit just to see what was going on every Sunday and Wednesday. Now we attend regularly and experience fellowship together as a family.

My husband used to make comments like, "for someone who does not have a job, you are so busy". I guess what he actually meant was since I wasn't working outside the home, I wasn't working. That would be reason enough to act like a nut around him, but I made the choice to ignore the comment. We all have a choice! We have a choice to shut our mouth. We do not have to have the last word. I learned to avoid conflicts by not saying one word! Every time we are challenged, whether wrong or right, we do not have to say anything. We can just walk away. Whenever I feel conflict coming on I tell my husband, "I am not going to entertain that right now." Our husbands couldn't handle half of what we do, and keep a sound mind. When our husbands come home, they should come home to a clean house, respectful children, and a dinner prepared as they like it. Now tell me this…if that isn't a job then what is?

Although we should have a balance in our marriages, there are certain things you may have to do to keep a balance. I set a limit on the amount of time we spend together when we go shopping, eating or touring a city. I do this to avoid an eruption that can come when we spend too much time together. As women we have to admit most men don't get into the shopping mood like we do. Men just can't take being in the same store, looking at the same item for a long time. So to avoid conflict, shorten your together time.

Does that mean you are letting him have his way? No, it means you will do what is necessary to keep your marriage happy and whole. There are times when I had to just say NO. No mall trips today! You have to do what you have to do. Let's be real. Now there are times we enjoy trips to the mall, stores and movies as a family and really have fun. My husband often tells me, "I really enjoyed our day together." But we had to work on getting to that point. I believe if we would be real and confront more issues in our life, and stop trying to look like something or someone we are not, we would grow to a capacity that we never thought we could.

One of the main reasons our husbands have such a hard time walking in a Godly role in the home is they had no leadership in the home. They had no examples to imitate, or role models to learn from - at least not in a Godly way. If we look at it this way, as if we accepted a job, but we had never been trained to do that job. How would we perform? Not well at all.

That is the problem with many husbands. They have never been properly trained. It is hard for a person to give up those old fleshly ways, but I tell you God can do what we will let him do. When a wife keeps her husband lifted up before the Lord, and encourages and supports him, she will have a great marriage. I pray daily for my husband to have the wisdom, guidance and understanding from God, not only for his home, but his job and in everything he deals with. Here is a prayer and confession you can pray over your spouse:

Ephesians 2: 17-18
That the God of our Lord Jesus Christ, the Father of glory, may give to (spouse name) the spirit of wisdom and revelation in the knowledge of him. The eyes of (spouse name) being enlightened; that (spouse name) may know what is the hope of his calling, what are the riches of the glory of His inheritance in the saints.

The Word works, if we work it! Yes, you will make mistakes, but you don't have stay there. You can pick up the ball and keep rolling. I do!

One of the main objectives in your marriage should be to live a Godly life, understand God, please him, respect him and always examine yourself.

Hebrews 11: 6 clearly shows us what we must have to please God - "But without faith, it is impossible to please Him, for he who comes to God must believe that He is, and that He is a rewarder of those who diligently seek Him.

Are you diligently seeking him? When you are seeking something, you are more than serious about getting results.

Things do not always happen in our marriage, our personal life, and even our dreams when we think they should. They happen in God's time. Now my husband is actively involved in our ministry. As he served his country as a Marine, God was preparing him for that role in his house as well. Many times God doesn't give us what we have been praying for because we are simply not ready for it. We have to mature and be developed in the things of God, and be prepared to handle situations as they come to us.

I heard one woman share that there was a man she talked to that said he thought he would help this cocoon, so he opened the cocoon. When he did, what he found was part worm and part cocoon. It just wasn't the right time yet.

Chapter Three

Children –A Heritage from the Lord

Our children are a valuable asset to all families. They are truly a gift from God. If you really think of the responsibility God gave us as parents, we should be honored that he would trust us with such gifts.

Proverbs 22:6 Train up a child in the way he should go, and when he is old he will not depart from it.

We must not let Satan use this scripture for his benefit. Whatever they are trained in, remember that is the way they will go.

When someone trusts you with something, they show that they value your opinion and decision making. We must not think one moment, that God wouldn't equip us with what we need to raise Godly children. No more dreaming of having Godly children. God has given us children to raise, guide, train and mold in his way. Believe me, you have been prepared. But like any job it takes prayer, preparation and training. When we follow God's word and pray we are being trained to be Godly parents. This brings more joy into our home.

As parents when we are not in our proper role as a parent, our children are left out to fend for themselves. Why do you think there are kids deciding to take other kids lives, and their own life, based on plain old hatred? The simple fact is that Satan has more time with our children than some of their parents do. We seem to have more faith in a 30-year mortgage than in our ability to be good parents! When we truly trust God, we don't hesitate to accept a job offer that is in our heart even if the money maybe less than another position we are interested in. God will set up a position just to lead us into one where the finances are there just as we desired. But we Must trust God! I know this for a fact. There have been a few jobs I thought I wanted. What I felt in my heart wasn't what the job had to offer. Surely God had another position with the salary, time, and flexibility that I desired.

Parents are so busy working, working and more working that there is no quality time to share with their children. As our children become teenagers, it is even more imperative to be there for them. Those hormones arrive, peer pressure comes upon them, and they just don't know what to do. I tell my girls, "As parents we are here for you." I talk with them about all the challenges that they will face in life. I explain how important their body is to them, and that virginity shouldn't be a dirty word. I let them come to me with questions and I give them the best answers that I can. Our children shouldn't get their advice from a peer of their same age. They are experiencing the same type's pressures and frustrations and can not provide answers the way a parent can.

We can't be shy with our kids, especially when it comes to sex and issues that may seem uncomfortable to discuss. We must let them know that their body's are as a temple of the Holy Spirit, and they must save themselves for a Godly husband. It is such an honor to God. We need to share with them God's way, before the enemy infiltrates their mind. We need to be an example to follow, so they will also see the realness of God almighty. Just because the infant and baby stage is over, our parenting job is no where near finished.

As mothers, we can take on a part-time job, or a temporary job to accommodate the family needs, but let's not do it at the cost of our children. One important thing--we must not create a lot of bills to burden our husbands, and expect them to take care of them graciously. We must keep a balance. There were times when money was so tight, I could hear it screaming, but I depended on God. God never let us down. Whenever I chose to work outside the home, it didn't bring conflict to our family's schedule.

I talk with many different women on a consistent basis. One particular lady I am acquainted with told me that she has put her career on hold for too long for the sake of her family. I told her "you are a wife and a mother, and that is a great responsibility". Our children need our love! Our children need our time! Our children need our attention!

I had the opportunity of talking to another young lady who has been through great stress in and out of her home, yet she still strives to get to her job to put in some hours. This lady has suffered injuries from two car accidents. She suffers with migraine headaches, and back pain but she honestly feels when she can go to work, she must put in her hours. I told her "your body and your children are more important than that job." I asked her why she continues to work while her body and her children suffer. I asked, "How does that profit you?" She looked at me with a glazed stare, shook her head and said nothing. Tell me who wins in that situation?

Showing our children that we love them and care for them opens a door of communication that we may have thought we could never have. Another important thing to remember is that we can be in our homes with our children and still not really be there. We can still get caught up in our jobs we may do in our homes, in our favorite videos or even those good old long phone calls. Sometimes I get caught up in what I am doing in the home and tune my girls out. I try to avoid doing this by taking time out to talk, laugh and joke around with my girls.

When my girls come home from school, we share the evening together. They do homework; have downtime, eat dinner and we chat. One good thing is that my daughters come home at two different times, so I have time to spend with one before being bombarded from the other. Things aren't always smooth, but I strive daily to make our time together better and better. Sometimes my girls think I am off my rocker, but I always try to do what is best for my girls. Of course as parents, we can't always be so good, and will have to ask for forgiveness. I am in no way perfect, and I continue to seek better ways of dealing with my children. The enemy would try to push a short fuse button in dealing with my girls. I continually pray about it, repent and learn to deal with my frustration from a different perspective. A lot of things we deal with have been brought into our family simply from un-repented sin from our forefathers - better known as a curse. And if these things aren't dealt with, they will carry from one generation to another. Whether it is alcoholism, adultery, lying, it doesn't matter - deal with it! These things will try to hide sometimes within one generation and then reappear into the next. Accept what you like, reject what you don't like, and is not God-like in your life. Confess it, ask for forgiveness and appropriate the blood of Jesus over that thing. You can do it! Here's the scripture: Pray it if you need to and trust God you are forgiven. We did!

1 John 1:9 If we confess our sins, He is faithful and just to forgive us our sins and to cleanse us from all unrighteousness. Make it personal here - ***I (Name) confess my sins, I believe God is faithful and just to forgive my sins and to cleanse me from all unrighteousness.***

As mothers, we must also have quality time for ourselves. I know as women, we tend to always have something to do or should I say find something to do? We must take time sometimes just to sit down. I tell my children if mom is praying, enjoying the Word – respect that time! I also remind them to read the Word and review scriptures.

We can take our children for granted so easily, because they are ours and they are always around. God is serious about us covering our children. We should enable and assist them in doing what we weren't able to do. We have to let them know they can do anything if they try. We have a responsibility to them.

Psalms 127: 3 Lo, children are a heritage of the Lord and the fruit of the womb is his reward.

I have always been a person that brings laughter to any situation. I try to keep joy and fun in our home. We must also keep laughter and joy in our hearts. My girls sometimes look at me as if I have lost it, but that is just the way I am. They think I am goofy, too silly, but they are used to it! I just simply enjoy having fun. I often share with them that there are plenty of children that would love to have their parents there for them, let alone laugh, joke and have a good time with them.

Although I enjoy having fun with my children, I had to start drawing the line on our playtime. I tended to get carried away when playing and I believe they forgot who the parent was. We should have fun, but we shouldn't step out of our role as a Godly parent. Children don't need us to be their buddies; they need us to be parents. They need us to be there to enforce and strengthen them against temptation and trouble. Good relationships are essential to help stabilize and salvage our children when the going gets tough. We have to accept each of our children as a person with his/her own individual personality. Each child can be so different. Our oldest daughter has a strong personality and she wants to make a statement on everything we say. We correct her on the spot and deal with it as a parent should. We tell her that this could be a great advantage later in life as an attorney, judge or politician. Our youngest daughter is different. She is willing to help a little more, ask what can she do and make sure things are carried out within the family quicker. Our children's attributes should be used for the kingdom of God to bring greatness in their life. For example, our oldest daughter's stronger personality is a plus for her because she handles any situation she may encounter very well. Now the youngest daughter will run in a heartbeat from any situation she encounters that takes her out of her comfort zone. Think about your own children's special attributes.

Consistency is necessary. Proper discipline brings lasting results to both child and parent.

Proverbs 22:15 *Foolishness is bound up in the heart of a child; the rod of correction will drive it far from him.*

Am I always consistent? No. But I try to correct myself. I found out that it is never too late to correct any measures of discipline. I don't beat myself up as I once did; I continually strive to be consistent in my ways of discipline. I also found out that every battle isn't worth fighting. I've learned how to deal with each situation differently. I came to realize that I don't need to fight every situation. Before, if the girls had clothes on the floor – I would say something. Now I don't think that battle is worth fighting. Now I let them know that they MUST have their rooms cleaned once a week. I don't care what day or what time, but it must get cleaned weekly. The clothes can hang from the ceiling everyday, but on that 7th day, that room better be cleaned or then the battle will begin! This is just one way to show our children we love them, and want the best for them. They tend to think we are out to get them when we use corrective measures, but I tell them we aren't out to get you, we are out to get something to you.

Too many children take life so easy; they don't know what it means to work hard. They are handed everything they want much too easy. This is a generation of excess. They want it all, and they want it now. According to "Teen Newsweek - October 11, 2004"; 30% of parents say that brand preference is of "major importance" to their kids. It is sad that many parents let the fade of the generation keep them in debt for their children. Is this only to impress? 75% of parents say their kids do fewer chores than children did 10 years ago according to this study. At the same time in 2003 12-19 year-olds roughly spent $175 billion, or $53 billion more than in 1997, according to Teen Research Unlimited. Some psychologists say that parents who overindulge their kids may be setting them up for future anxiety and depression. Recent studies show that kids who were given too much too soon often have difficulty coping with life's disappointments as adults according to this article.

In allowing our children to work less and get more, I believe is a big set up for them later in life. We must show discipline in every area of our life. Whether you decide to spank or not, you must make a quality decision that discipline will sometimes hurt the parent, so it must always be done in love. When you think about saving a soul from hell, read this scripture.

Proverbs 23:13-14 do not withhold correction from a child, for if you beat him with a rod he will not die.

You shall beat him with a rod, and deliver his soul from hell. A lot of us have disciplined our children in a way without realizing why we did it. When our children asked us why we make decisions concerning them, our famous answer is, "because I told you so". Now what kind of answer is that? We have to be open and honest with our children so that we do not give the enemy any room to infiltrate.

We also have to be careful not to repeat negative ways that were shown to us. There were times I had to look at myself and ask, "Were my grandmother and mothers" ways Godly?" I had to try to correct my negative attitudes so I would not carry them to a new generation.

2 Corinthians 10:4 for the weapons of our warfare are not carnal but mighty in God for pulling down strongholds.

    Whether we are dealing with anger, frustration or impatience, God's Word has an answer for it. We have to have the determination to renew our mind and make a change. One thing that can really hit hard is when you look at your children, and just see yourself in the mirror. Boy, that's deep. I know it is so easy to say that certain things run in the family. Well I challenge you with the Word of God, to run them right out of your life.

    In this time of learning, much knowledge is exposed to us. We are truly living in the later days, and you can see it with all the disruption and disrespect that children have toward their parents, and our society. God is raising up men and women of God who are preaching and teaching bolder than ever before. If your family doesn't base its life on our Lord and Savior Jesus Christ, there will never be pure joy in your home.

    However we are not here on a joy ride, just passing through. But we are here to serve the Lord, and instill in our children the importance of serving the Lord, our Savior. As parents, the Lord is trusting in us to care for our children. We are to be good stewards over our children. We are to be good stewards over everything God has blessed us with.

    I come across many children that not only do not know the Lord, but their parents have no knowledge of God, and they show no reverence or respect for the Lord in the home. It hurts me to see these kids who are headed for destruction because of the ignorance of their parents. One thing I ask—"are there bad kids or bad parents?" Something recently disturbed me when I was in a grocery store. I saw a child about two years old, in a buggy, drop a bottle of baby food on the floor. Of course, it broke and right in the middle of a busy isle. The adult with the child (not sure if it was his mother), was looking away at something else. When she finally noticed the mess, she just walked away and told the child that someone else will clean it up. Glass was in the middle of the isle, and people had to be told to watch it and be careful. I couldn't believe it. I proceeded to contact someone who could clean it up. Now what does that example show our children? It shows them not to take pride in the community around them. Most of all it shows them disrespect and will desensitize them to people when they are in need. Parents must realize they are going to be held accountable for leading their children down the wrong path in life. We must teach and lead our children by example.

Another difficult topic today is dating. I have talked with children whose parents allow them to date at a very young age. What is the reasoning for allowing a child between the ages of 11-15 to become so active in a romantic relationship? I believe this causes emotions to be flared up in our children that they are not going to be able to manage. They should not be confronted with adult situations. Why rush them through their youth? Let them know they should enjoy this period of their life. It is no wonder why children are failing tests, losing sleep, losing weight and becoming frustrated. I hear of middle-schoolers that are involved in relationships and I believe this teaches our youth that marriage is not sacred. Hey- you can leave one relationship if you don't like it, and seek another. Too bad they don't know that once you get out of one relationship, part of that person is still a part of you. Can you imagine if a child started dating at 11 years old, and had several relationships a year. By the age of 18, there are too many parts of too many people incorporated in their heart.

We have shared with our daughters that they will not be allowed to date in their early teen years. We stress to them the importance of concentrating on their studies, and on focusing on what they want to be when they grow up. I have told them dating is to some degree a preparation for marriage. I ask them "are you preparing for marriage?" I don't think so! In time, the right time for dating will unfold!

Today's world offers the wrong kind of fun to our children and if we go along with it we are exposing them to great evil. Our world today offers up sex, drinking, pornography and much, much more to our children. They should be above those things, and behave as children of God. They should not be open to seduction by the enemy. Pray over your children daily, especially before they leave home for school. My girls and I pray each morning before they go to school. I also confess the Parents' Prayer (that is at the end of this message) regularly over our girls. Again…confession brings possession. Speak blessings over your children, so they will not be caught up and bound to the foolishness in this world.

We have to point our children in the right direction, give them the right goals to strive for. I ask God to show me the gift within my girls, so I can help them achieve their gifts. We should all have goals we strive for in our daily lives. God didn't put us here to look good; he put us here for a mission. We are on a mission of raising a Godly family and reaching lost souls. God has put dreams in each and every one of us, and it is entirely up to us as to what we will do with those dreams.

How badly do you want to realize your dreams? Are you willing to let people talk you out of it? What if Thomas Edison had given up his dream after being labeled retarded? How about J.C. Penney? J. C. Penney was told the best job he could have would be on a farm. Do you know that Albert Einstein failed high school Algebra? There are endless stories of people who were told to limit their dreams but went on to be great successes. It is the same for our children and for us, we can realize our dreams.

It hurts me to see families treat their children as if they have no value.

Matthew 18:3 Assuredly, I say to you, unless you are converted and become as little children, you will by no means enter the kingdom of heaven.

Can you imagine not entering heaven, because you treated your children as if they had no worth? I can't.

We must become as children: trusting, faithful, and honest. If we took greater notice of our children, I believe we could learn more than we ever realized was possible. Children hold nothing back. They will tell you the truth in a heartbeat. Sometimes when my children share things with me, it may cut me and sometimes I take it personally. But I have realized that if it's tight it must be right. My children made me realize that I had to start working on changes I needed to make. Most times when our children are doing things that we don't like, all we have to do is look in the mirror.

Remember that change has to start within ourselves. Many times when I thought my children were provoking situations, it was not them, it was me.

Ephesians 6:4 and you fathers, do not provoke your children to wrath, but bring them up in the training and admonition of the Lord.

Wow, how hard it was for me to swallow that? Talk about pride. I realized how I was confusing my children with what I was telling them. When I took a close look, I noticed that even the dog was confused about what I was saying. We have to be real in our life. You can't change unless you are honest with yourself. People like folks who are real, who share real feelings, real situations, and real results!

I also know the enemy will use your children to create strife, confusion and frustration. We must deal with problems on the spot. I realize siblings fuss and have disagreements, but there should be a limit. Many times I remove myself from the situation so I won't get heated up. I save myself a lot of trouble by letting my husband step in and take over. Instead of always repeating myself with—"clean up your room," "fold the clothes," "do the dishes," I said nothing. When my husband noticed that chores were not being done, he stepped in. One word from Dad and the chores were attended to right away. He threatened to take money away from their allowances. Now that got their attention, most of the time. As mothers we help our children a little more than their Dads. A mother is there to help her kids with what they are doing, but dad is going to give the instructions and expect it to get done. That's just the way it is! We all know that when it all comes down to it—most of the time children are going to look for Mom.

I have the opportunity to work with teenagers in our local school system, and it really surprises me how many of them have never attended church. I know nothing should surprise me, but golly! I also learned that some kids went to church, but never had the Lord Jesus Christ introduced to them. That is where I felt I needed to assist--to have talks with them about the Lord when the opportunity came up. I have had the pleasure of taking some to church with me, and several accepted the Lord Jesus Christ. Now how much is that worth?

I am so thankful my children accepted the Lord in their younger years. I can't imagine being without the Lord in our home. Talk about unspeakable joy.

Romans 15:13 now may the God of hope fill you with all joy and peace in believing, that you may abound in hope by the power of the Holy Spirit.

As parents we must make sure we are in good standing with God, because if we are not it will only bring on destruction to our children. If parents would realize they have to stand before God, and give an account of what they did or did not share with their children, they would take God's word more seriously. I am so thankful my husband and I accepted Christ when our children were small. Because they were so young, they have always known about the Lord in our home. If we hadn't been saved my husband and I would have had to try to get rid a lot of ungodly truths that would have been built into them. Even as a Christians, would we do things differently? Most definitely so. We should always be open for change in our lives, to make life better.

Yes, I know there are families out there who are doing well and have great children. But how will they measure the success of their children? Will it be by how big a house they have, how nice their car is, or what college degree they earn? There is nothing wrong with any of that, but what it all comes down to is, do their children love the Lord? Are we sometimes sacrificing our children for the pursuit of money?

I have asked God to forgive me for the ways I have acted or things I have said to my children that weren't in line with the Word. I try daily to achieve another level of understanding with my girls. Again, I say the enemy knows the weaknesses we have and will ponder and try to expose those areas in our lives. We have to continually let him know he is defeated, and no matter how much he tries to bring guilt into our lives, he is a liar!

Remember a lot of issues that come up in our lives are simply curses that have not been dealt with. As a believer we have the right and authority to cast those things out in Jesus' name.

Whether it is a sickness, infirmity, weakness, phobias, etc., we have authority to command that thing to go.

Luke 10:19 Behold I give you the authority to trample on serpents and scorpions, and over all the power of the enemy, and nothing shall by any means hurt you.

We must continually confess the Word of God over that thing, until it has manifested in the natural.

We have to make good choices for our children. When we put our job's first, the home we desire, the lovely car, we sometimes put our children last. Material things should not be as important as our children. When we put our jobs, fine car and big house first, we open the door to Satan to influence our children, and invite them into situations that eventually lead them into destruction. Do we want to be responsible for sending our children to hell? I don't think so! Well that is what we do when we choose material things over spending time with our children and family as God desires us to do. Do not get me wrong; there is nothing wrong with the nice home, the nice car, but we must prioritize our lives. God said;

Deuteronomy 8:18, for it is he who gives us power (ability) to get wealth.

We have settled for the old tale that it takes two people working outside the home to make it. That is a lie and trick of the enemy, Satan, so he can always have his hand in the family plan.

John 10:10 the thief does not come except to steal, and to kill, and to destroy.

Oh I hear some of you say "yeah, but my children turned out fine," and others say "we are doing well with our schedules." I don't doubt one bit that their children are fine and they have a great relationship. A lot of times I see the lifestyle and it is not a lifestyle that is good for the Lord. We have other friends who are living for the Lord and their children are doing well, but the schedule they keep and the hustle & bustle they contend with makes me doubt that there is total fulfillment in their lives. I know some of them desire to eliminate their hectic schedules. I know several people that have to get their children up at 4:30 and 5:00am so they can get to work on time. Come on now, what kind of schedule is that for our children?

Do you actually think it was God's plan for children to spend 10 to12 hours a day in childcare or in school away from their parents? Do you think God intended for children to come home from school to an empty home for 2 to 4 hours a day while both parents are still at work? Do you think it was God's plan to allow children to have so much free time on their hands between the hours of 3 to 6pm? What joy is possible in such a home? Not a lot. This simply allows Satan himself--to infiltrate, and penetrate our children. That is why it is so important for a mother to be there for her children, go to their school, and have lunch with them. Fathers should do this as well. Our children really enjoy when their dad does something with them. You can't be with them 24/7 but you should do all you can whenever you are with them. There are companies now that allow their employees an hour a week off their job, to spend time with their children at school. What message does that send? It sends out a message that it is time to stop pushing our children to the side. Again, I will admit I don't have it all together as a mother, but I strive daily to be better. I have asked God to help me improve all areas of being a good mother.

We must keep our children in prayer daily, for the simple fact that the world sends too many mixed messages to them. We all get the message that we need, "gun control, movie control, music control", but on the other end, the world says "spanking is an unacceptable form of discipline". And we wonder why our children are killing; have no respect for each other or for adults. The bible says clearly the rod of correction lies in our hand.

Proverbs 22:15 *Foolishness is bound up in the heart of a child; the rod of correction will drive it far from him*.

Now who are we going to believe, a world where mass confusion and violence are overtaking our children, or in God the creator of us all?

Our children are looking for too much power from such things as Pokeman, Dragonball Z and Harry Potter. These programs and movies are direct targets on our youth's minds. They feel that if they can gain power they will be something special. They do not understand that they were created in the image of God and are already special. These things not only teach about having power, but witchcraft, sorcery and spells. And we wonder what is wrong with our youth. These things are also replacing the valuable family time that we should be sharing together.

After taking prayer away from our schools, there is nothing left but trouble. We have now given Satan an open target for our youth. A lot of us are rebelling. We won't submit. Our kids won't submit. And we want to still hear from God. Let me give you a revelation: God is not in the midst of confusion. I work in a school and I see many parents addressing schoolteachers and leaders in authority with disrespect. They challenge their suggestions and disciplinary measures for their children. Now what does that teach our children? There are children in our society we have to deal with that brings hate and discontent into our schools. Those of us who are Christians must stand firm, flatfooted and face the enemy head on. We have to tell Satan that they he is a LIAR and we will not let him destroy our children or our families. The Bible gives us many applications for our daily life. God has given us authority over these satanic forces. Satan is a defeated foe. We must exercise our authority daily!

Luke 10:19 Behold, I give you the authority to trample on serpents and scorpions, and over all the power of the enemy, and nothing shall by any means hurt you.

Read this scripture several times, and let it penetrate. There is no excuse for us to be out of our authority. We are out of our authority, for the simple reason, that we want to be.

When we put the Bible first in our lives, and let the Word of God be the final authority in our life, we can't help but win. So many Christian families tend to compromise and when they do, they open up the door for the enemy to come in. Some have the nerve to say; well I didn't get to party, go to the club, and watch certain movies, so I don't want to shelter my kids from that. What do you want to do? Open the door to hell. That is what you are leading your kids to. I get so tired of hearing compromising

Christians. Some even have the nerve to live in sin, and attend Church faithfully. Boy, talk about playing with fire. These same Christians are the ones who often attack the other sinners. They constantly deal with many frustrations with no victory. As believers staying consistently in prayer, will eliminate the enemy from attempting to bring trouble to us. Oh he will continue to try but it is crucial to never give in. Engulf your children in prayer, teach them the word, live a holy life. Keep positive things before them because the enemy will stay at his game. It is amazing that after you teach all this, there will still be negativity and temptations at their door. See why prayer is so important?

Working in a school where I had contact with children made me even more aware of what I needed to do as a parent. More than 50% of high school students have experienced drugs and sex and continue to do so. What is even sadder is that middle school and elementary school students are experimenting with these same things. Why? Because no one is there to talk to them, to love them and guide them. Some children told me that they thought when they got married and had children then they would start attending church with their children. How sad. I explained to them that you need to know the Lord yourself and then you are ready to bring your children up in the Lord.

Thank God for teachers and our public schools, because I tell you our children would miss out on a lot more if they weren't there. There have been a lot of hurtful attacks on public educators according to Forrest J. "Frosty" Troy, editor, radio and television commentator, critic, humorist and one of the most dynamic public speakers in the country. He is recognized nationally for his upbeat presentations on public education. In an era of weasel words and budget cuts, Frosty Troy is a blunt, dynamic defender of public education. He ought to know. He's been in the trenches for 30 years, fighting for decent funding and public support for education from the precincts of his hometown to the corridors of power in Washington.

Frosty shares - the most painful one is the charge that public schools are "Godless" institutions of secularism. The Constitution requires that public education be neutral in religious education, but that's a far cry from the debasement heaped upon public educators.

Because teachers can't pin on a church label and baptize the students doesn't make public education any less spiritual. It isn't the babbling critics who wrap themselves in religious intolerance who are making a difference for all of God's children. They preach to the saved in the rear echelon while public school teachers staff the front line.

Who is for spiritual values for kids and who is just kidding? Can you name any other institution that comes nearer to biblical injunctions than our public schools?

Feeding the hungry – Over 30% of public school children have their only hot meal at school.

Clothing the naked – There's hardly an elementary school in poor neighborhoods that don't have a clothing closet.

The widows' mite – The average teacher spends over $400 of personal funds for school supplies for students.

Visiting prisoners – Public educators are manning the GED, vo-tech, literacy and skill centers behind prison walls.

No greater love – The Littleton teacher who guided children into a room for safety, and shielded them with his own body was shot in killed in front of the praying children.

Suffer the little ones – Who takes millions of retarded, disabled or mentally handicapped? Who redeems the dispossessed and the delinquent in alternative education programs?

Look who comes to public school among the 46.5 million enrolled this year, then consider who truly does God's work:

- Six million for whom English is a second language.
- Six million special education children.
- More than two million abused children.
- Nearly 500,000 from no permanent address—the homeless ones.

- One out of four comes from extreme poverty, are often born out of wedlock and many are abused, neglected, unwashed, unwanted and unloved.

You want heroes?

For millions of kids, the hug they get from a teacher is the only hug they will get that day because the nation is living through the worst parenting in history. Many have never been taken to church or synagogue in their lives.

A Michigan principal moved me to tears with the story of her attempt to rescue a badly abused little boy who doted on a stuffed animal on her desk - one that said, "I love you!" He said he'd never been told that at home.

This is a constant in today's society - two million unwanted, unloved, abused children in public schools, the only institution that takes them all in.

Teachers strive to find the best in their students, even where some see little hope. No other American bestows a finer gift than teaching - reaching out to the brilliant and the retarded, the gifted and the average.

Teachers leave the world a little bit better than they found it... They are America's unsung heroes. If you're looking for values check the majority of teachers who spend their time and money mentoring students, sponsoring non-academic activities while attempting to deal with the most undisciplined generation ever to enter public schools.

The public school day may not start with a Hail Mary or an Our Father, a mantra or a blood sacrifice, but public education does more of God's work every day than any other Institution in America—and that includes the churches – concludes Frosty!

Thank God for Holy Ghost filled teachers! They have to contend with parents who have the nerve to address administrative authority on issues that come up regarding their child. We must do better as parents. We cannot let any generation be taken at the hands of the enemy.

All our children want is to be shown that they are loved. When they are not shown this, they look for love in all the wrong places. That is how they end up in gangs and relationships that are bad for them. The simple fact is they were looking for love. Let's love our children right into Heaven! These are our future leaders who will bring great success to our country and our nation.

Chapter Four

Achieving Victory as a Single Mother

Single mothers have what I believe is a very great challenge. One of every four American children now lives in a single-parent home. So not only do a lot of mothers have the responsibility of a mother, they must also be the provider for the household and play the role of a father. Although she can't fill the shoes of a man and share from the perspective of a man, she can give great lessons and share insight to enhance her children's lives. Just showing love and nurturing children is the greatest task of being a mother. Balancing your family and career takes adjusting, but it can be done. A Mom that does it all can successfully combine workdays and parental duties. Good planning can allow a child raised in a single-parent home to do just as well as in a two-parent home.

God has not forgotten the single mothers and you must not let discouragement, depression or stress take over. Your children need you to guide and direct them, so you have no time to waste. Every time a thought of depression or loneliness tries to make its way in, think of your life and how valuable you are.

Jeremiah 29:11 for I know the plans I think toward you; says the Lord, thoughts of peace and not of evil, to give you a future and a hope.

Whenever depression is allowed into your life, it is a sure sign you have allowed your spirit to become empty. You have to believe what's inside of you. And that is greatness. We were all created for greatness. It is up to us what we will do with it. To cure that problem of emptiness, we must feed our spirit with the Word of God. Each and every one of us was uniquely and wonderfully created and has a destiny and purpose to fulfill on this earth. Now it is up to us to fulfill it. God didn't create robots; he gave each and every one of us a free will. He also gave us the choice of choosing life or death.

Deuteronomy 30:19 I call heaven and earth as witnesses today against you, that I have set before you life and death, blessing and cursing; therefore choose life, that both you and your descendents may live.

God even gives us the answer to the test. We make the choice for our children.

Single motherhood is what you make of it. It can be full, rich and rewarding or an existence of self-pity, low self-esteem and even depression. You have to accept who you are; a special person from the hand of the creator. Give thanks for what has become of your life and always, I mean always, think of the good things in your life. There will be times of disappointment, but you will make it through it all. Don't criticize and put yourself down. Remember God is a forgiving God. Always speak good things. Even if things may not be going as you desire, remember God has a plan and purpose for your life. Keep a good attitude. Don't feel sorry for yourself.

The following suggestions may be helpful in helping you deal with your every day life:

- Organize your financial situation. Learn how to live by a budget. If you need help, find some help in the area you live.
- Seek out help from government programs such as: grants, subsidies..Etc. If you can't find a job, there are many programs to assist you in your time of need such as: Women, Infants, and Children (WIC), Aid to Families with Dependent Children (AFDC). There are also programs with Head Start for younger children as well. Check with your pediatrician, family and friends.

As a single mother, you can't feel you have been a failure. Below you will find just a few suggested ideas to help you in living from day to day.

- Keep your children on a regular schedule. Any sudden changes can cause stress on your children.
- Try to spend a little quality time each day with your child. It goes a long way.
- Ask your child about their feelings. If you need help, seek out a professional for them. Also if you are part of a local ministry, talk with your pastor.
- Keep discipline in your home. This involves teaching your child appropriate ways of behaving. Let them know right off the bat, what is acceptable and expected.
- Find time to yourself. Call upon a trusted family member or friend so that you can enjoy an evening out. Whether it is alone or with friends.

You can be single and satisfied. We have all been in situations that have not turned out the way we desired. One thing we must remember as the old saying goes--winners never quit; and quitters never win! Being single may cause you to feel alone. You have a purpose in this life. I heard one illustration with keys on a ring. Each key is uniquely cut for its own purpose, but it's together on a ring with many other keys. It has a purpose, and so do you! When you have high self-esteem and continually involve yourself in outside activities you will pull yourself out of any loneliness that tries to come upon you. Joining a local church that teaches the word of God, with no compromise is crucial for your life. Finding fellowship with other women will make a great difference in your life. Find a mentor, someone you admire and respect. This person should be one who rules their home well, who has values that you see them walking out in life. I have shared some websites in this message that I feel will provide great information for you.

Being a single mother I know your time may feel stretched, but I tell you we mothers have been specially equipped. I tell you, even as a married woman, I was pulled and stretched I believe to the fullest. When my girls needed to get to a basketball practice, basketball game, soccer practice, soccer game, or any other after school activity I was there. Boy, talk about a neighborhood taxi. My husband was rarely available for these things because of his job schedule.

Whatever situation that brought you to be a single parent; you must not allow bitterness, anger, rejection or guilt to take root in you. These can be detrimental not only to your health but also your guidance and teaching as a parent. Your children need you to have a sound mind. We must always remember, if God is so willing to forgive us, we must be able to forgive others and ourselves. Don't allow unnecessary stress to come upon your children. At this time in their life they need someone that is focused and established in their life.

I know it may be a little harder to be more involved in your children's lives during school time or activities. Try to drop a simple note to their teachers to show that you care and that you are paying attention. Make an arrangement to have lunch with them occasionally. That makes a great difference in their lives. I realize after awhile our children tend to be shy when parents are around. Seems like once they hit middle-school age, it is over. Kiss the lunch dates good-bye. They truly drop you like it's hot! If that is the case, have lunch and share a brief moment with them. Drop a simple love note in their lunch bag. Just something to show them you care. Single moms can be just as involved in their children's activities as with two parents in the house. Finding that balance will give you the opportunity to spend as much time as possible with your children. It is proven that children tend to do much better when parents show some type of involvement in their schools. The main thing is--let them know we care.

During your time at home with your children, instead of spending too much time watching TV, join in a conversation with them, find out about school events and different things that may have gone on throughout the day. Don't be too shy to discuss sex, drugs, and choices of life for them. Its better you share insight with them, than having them get information from the streets. One thing for sure, you must monitor not only their activities and involvement's, but their friendships. To this day as my girls are 13 and 15 years old, I involve myself with whomever they call friends. While working in a school I was able to hear and see many things that in young people's behavior that I disapprove of. They may think we are goofy, but we have a responsibility to them, to not let them bring shame upon our homes.

Even if you do not have children, apply these principles to your own life and I believe you will find true fulfillment!

Here are some websites that are great resources for networking with other single women. You will find uplifting and enlightening information. The views on these sites are not necessarily the opinion of the author.

www.womenoffaith.com
Women of Faith is an interdenominational women's ministry committed to helping women of all faiths, backgrounds, age groups, and nationalities. **Women of Faith** was founded specifically to meet the needs of women. They are committed to helping women grow emotionally, spiritually and in relationships: whether in marriages, friendships, the workplace or with their children.

www.singlemomz.com
Single Momz offers support and information to women dealing with issues such as child support, custody and divorce.

www.singlemothering.com
Single Mothering is a support group for single moms. **SingleMothering** has been online since 1998. The mission is to provide a supportive networking community for single moms of all ages in a positive forum.

www.singlemothers.org
Single Mothers is dedicated to helping single moms meet the challenges of daily life with wisdom, wit, dignity, confidence and courage since 1991. Whether a mother is outside of marriage by choice or chance, pregnant, or divorced, adoptive or widowed, they will be at home here!

www.SheLovesGod.com
She Loves God is a support community for Christian women - read/submit articles, inspirational stories, & poems. This is a

Christian support community helping you progress from whatever stage you at are spiritually.

www.bringinghope.net
Bringing Hope offer programs for single moms with life skills to increase self-esteem and self-sufficiency find resources and gain emotional support. There is no investment of money, just your time, commitment and effort.

www.generationmoms.com
Generation Mom helps moms achieve work, life and balance by using the Internet to find flexible, telecommuting and freelance work and outsource work at home.

www.thebabycorner.com
The Baby Corner is a community for expectant and new parents for babies and toddlers. **Baby Corner** provides quality information, advice, and a community for expectant and new parents.

www.cwahm.com
CWAHM.com The online magazine for Christian Work at Home Moms ... The ezine for Christian work at home moms. Here you'll find resources to uplift you, encourage you, and help you find a great work at home job and many other features!

www.singlerose.com
Single Rose is a resource for single mothers on the web. **Single Rose** is an emotionally supportive publication for divorced, widowed and never married women raising children alone.

www.momsrefuge.com
Moms Refuge offers refuge! Life to Hectic? Come on in and find refuge. Supportive parent and women's community featuring discussion and advice from both experts and working mothers.

www.singleparentsonline.net

Single Parents Online is a resource of shared experiences by single mothers and fathers. One this site you will find special sections geared toward single parents plus a chat board with stories, tips, comments and questions from other single parents.

www.singleparentsnetwork.com
Single Parents Network mission is to provide a hub, as you will, that has collectively gathered other web sites, articles, information and support boards and so much more, for anyone looking for single parent information.

www.singlemotherssupportnetwork.org
Single Mothers Support Network nourishes the roots of our society. The single mothers support network believes that the job of a mother or father raising a child is perhaps the most important in our society.

www.singlewahm.com
The Christian Work at Home Mom – A guide to get you started! Here you'll share stories and look for special ways to support each other in home businesses.

Chapter Five

The Complete Homemaker!

When most of us hear about a job, we think about a job in the 9 to 5 working world. Who thinks about the job a wife and mother does daily? As mothers, we don't have a job description laid out in front of us, but we do know we are more than qualified for each position we encounter daily. We have become so accustomed to thinking that the only important job is a career in the corporate world. We forget about the most important job, that of being a wife and mother. Most of us want to be out in the world where all the "so-called action" is. Not only are many mothers outside of the home, many women are raising children without fathers. The social norm has changed drastically as the enemy pushes people into ungodly relationships.

We must get our information from God, not the world. That may be our problem. We keep seeking the world's opinions, and talk-show opinions, instead of seeking God's opinions. When we heed to those worldly opinions, we open the door to Satan's domain. When we get out of the order of God, we get into trouble. Look at our world today.

I am not denouncing anyone who works outside of the home, because God places us in many situations at different seasons in our lives. One thing I do know is working inside or outside of the home, we must stand firm and strong on our Christian ethics and not allow our environment to change our views. You have to listen to your calling as wife and mother. I do know when you accept the important role of wife and mother; your life should change to accommodate your family's needs.

The title home worker is an honored title. A home worker is productive.

Titus 2:4-5 that they admonish the young women to love their husbands, to love their children, to be discreet, chaste, homemakers, good, obedient to their own husbands, that the word of God may not be blasphemed.

Why is it that Christian and non-Christian women have left their homes for a career? 1) Women are not being instructed clearly in the Word of God. Women have been encouraged to drift with the culture. 2) They think that to be a woman of importance you have to be out there in the working world. The result is a lot of what is going on in our homes. We have more broken homes, rebellious children; kids shooting kids, kids crying out 'somebody love me'! Right now marriages are failing at the rate of over 50%. Over 60% of our children are being raised in single family homes. We even have teenage couples taking their own lives, simply because they can't abide by their parents rules.

When we stay home, we are not trapped. We have to build friendships, attend a local church which supports women's fellowship and join local support groups for women. That way we won't feel left out. We must go after our passions and desires in the home. If you are like me, the list of things to do never ends. You may think; how do I have time to think about a passion or desire? If you care and desire to be the best mom and wife you can be, you will find a way. Arrange a day that you and your spouse can agree on where you can spend time alone. Whether it is out with special friends or just time to yourself, it will make a difference in how you handle day to day.

I suggest right here you take time out to write a simple letter to yourself. Ask yourself what in life do you desire for you and your family? In that letter write out goals, dreams and visions. Be reasonable with your timing of your goals. Don't feel pressured in feeling you have to do it quickly. Whether you feel you can accomplish it in one month, one year or 5 years. Be realistic. And most of all if you don't make your goal schedule don't make yourself feel like you are a failure. You are not!! Pick up the ball and start rolling again. If it was so easy, everyone would be doing it. You can!

When you do something you enjoy for yourself, you will feel better about yourself. Pursuing your own self-interests will also make you feel better about yourself. Maybe you don't know how to find what your interest is--well consider things that were important to you in the past or are important now. You must continue to pursue your dreams. If you have to, you may have to revisit your dreams. Each and every one of us has a dream of greatness inside of us waiting to be born. Don't lose your dreams. Spend time praying and meditating. Make a list of your dreams and passions. This may help you discover what you need to concentrate on. Each of us is uniquely made. What you desire to do the most, what gives you a great passion, I challenge you to cultivate and develop it. Realizing your dream will bring the fulfillment in your life. Just because you may have an encounter when pursuing your dreams, don't let it go. People tend to give up when they faced with adversity. Again, don't lose your fire.

Most people are so unhappy with their jobs, simply because they are not passionate about what they do. You will never enjoy something, you don't love. Myles Monroe, a great man of God emphasized that one of the richest places in the world is the cemetery. That is because so many people didn't pursue their dreams and passions and died with them left in their heart. When it looks bad, we must believe. I can't express this enough – if it was so easy, everybody would be doing it. You must remember:

2 Cor 5:7 For we walk by faith, not by sight.

Sometimes finding your dreams might be easy. There may be a talent you once entertained. It is not as hard as you think. Take me for an example; I have worked with and around children for a long time. I have operated my own in-home childcare business as well. I have always felt a passion for children. I truly know this is in my heart. I look forward in arriving at the school I work at, and often stay a bit later. My girls think I am nuts, but I truly love working with our youth. Many call me "Mom" or "Auntie", while on the job. This just shows the nature and character I represent when I'm in their presence.

Whatever you desire and have compassion for, I can almost guarantee you can make a success out of it. If you don't like what you do for a living, how can you possibly be successful at it? You may want to consider new ideas. We are never too old for new ideas. How about inventing something? Have you ever seen something newly invented and said 'Oh I thought of that'? Well the thing that carried those inventors to success was that they followed their dreams, and you have to do it yourself. You can't rely on your husband or children to make your dreams come true. You have to believe in yourself! Remember you have to speak and confess what you desire to happen in your life. No one else will.

You may not have had a dream a year ago, remember one thing each year there should be growth in your life. That growth will cause new ventures to come your way. Wisdom is the key thing to any adventure.

Proverbs 4: 7 Wisdom is the principal thing; therefore get wisdom. And in all your getting get understanding.

It is how we apply the knowledge that we have learned. Your faith will also take you where you want to go, after all, it is impossible to please God without it. You can do anything if you really want it. If you can believe it, you can achieve it!

When you find your dream or passion, you'll wonder how I can find time to pursue it. Well, you have to make time, because time won't find you. Each and every one of us gets the same amount of time every day; the important thing is how we adjust to that time. One pastor I know stresses is to focus on removing hectic schedules from our lives. What purpose do they serve? Nothing. What will happen is you will become frustrated, procrastinate, and allow people to control your life. I made changes to my schedule. Instead of always being busy, I decided to slow down. There are weeks where it may be pretty busy, but it wasn't a pattern anymore. A lot of times, God can't speak clearly to us because we are too busy to hear the voice of the Lord. We can't do that. When you are home with your children and need time to get away, consider a book club, a visit to your local library, a membership in a local gym. Another great resource to help buy time is to share babysitting. Trade babysitting time with family and friends. There are also many childcare centers that offer hourly fees as well as daily or weekly. Take advantage of those! If you decide to work in your home, remember there will be early mornings and late nights you may have to spend while you get established. But always think of the reward--your family. If you have young children, you will have to arise before they wake up to get some work done; work while they nap; and work after they go to bed. Once you establish your business, or whatever you decide to do, before you know it, you won't have to put as much time into it. You will be able to go from possibly 10-12 hours per day, down to 6-8 hours per day.

Make sure you include your spouse in your decisions. He may not feel as adamant as you, but his support is critical in helping you achieve your goals. You must feel good about what you are doing so you will feel you deserve this time. Don't feel guilty about enjoying time just for yourself! That is a mind game you can do without. As mothers and wives we give great strength to our family and we should not be cheated out of our own dreams. Whatever your dreams or interests, there are many resources available that can help you achieve what you desire. All of the work-at-home resources shared in this book can help you attain your goals.

These women have put much time and effort into their businesses, and I continue to get great help from them to this day. Here is one book in particular that I will recommend. Cheryl Gochnauer – "So You Want to Be a Stay-at-Home Mom?"
This book tells you what being a stay-at-home mom is like from the perspective of one who is doing it. Step-by-step practical tips show how you can make the change. In this book you'll learn how to -evaluate your financial situation - find ways to live better on less - keep up on your career skills so you can return to the workforce - plan creative activities with your kids and get the support and encouragement you need.

Being the type of person I am, I always have to have something to do when my husband is involved with other things. I never sit around and have a pity party. People get depressed and feel alone because they have allowed a void to fill them. They give up on themselves. You must be confident in yourself, and strive for your full potential. As a Marine there were times when my husband was gone for long periods of time. Again, I made sure the girls and I stayed busy. My girls and I were either with friends or attending local community events or church activities. It is imperative to have a life that makes you feel complete, and you must make enjoying life a priority. That old saying, "life is not fair" is overused by many people. One thing I share with them is that life is what you make it! The choice is yours.

When a family makes a choice of a mother being in the home, it means a change of living habits, striving towards a realistic budget and sticking to it. Believe me, it takes work to get to that point, but there is nothing too hard for us. If we can dream it, we can achieve it. We must strive and work hard if we want to succeed. Mix this with faith and the Word of God and you can't go wrong.

If we are working outside of the home, we have to make sure we are recognized as a Godly woman. We must not compromise our Godly values. Let's be a better wife, mother and friend, so that we can impact the communities we live in, and better the kingdom of God. Even when we come home, we must bring the joy of the Lord with us. Never let the world take your joy away.

A new generation of career women, say they are less inclined to juggle career and motherhood at this time, according to Des Moines Register – "Family now, career later article, 8/5/01". The high-stress, have-it all attitudes are being replaced in many younger women with a belief that career and family should be taken one at a time. A lot of mothers are just maxed out! Some younger women are watching older women and saying, "I don't want my life to be like that." The number of children who are cared for by their married mothers at home while their fathers work has grown significantly over recent years, according to the latest Census Bureau.

According to "Time" dated 3/22/04, a lot of moms are caught between the pressures of the workplace and the demands of being a mom, more women are sticking with the kids.

The percentage of working women with infants fell recently for the first time since government began tracking the rise of mothers in the labor force nearly three decades ago. No matter how you slice it, more mothers are enjoying the slower pace and are able to answer the simple questions their children ask. Despite many sayings, a lot of the women that step out of their careers find expected delights on the home front, not to mention the enormous relief of no longer worrying about shortchanging their kids.

Where there is a choice many women with children are choosing motherhood. A lot are simply staying in the home until their children reach school age. Some women choose part-time work or projects to do in their home. Other women choose to job share. That means they share their job responsibilities with another person. This allows them to work only 2 or 3 days per week, giving them quality time to spend with family.

Experts say the new figures do not forecast a mass retreat of women from the workplace. If anything, they contend, it reflects the sense among many women that their place in the workforce is here to stay, and they can leave temporarily, without losing too much ground professionally.

A study by Catalyst found that 1 in 3 women with M.B.A's. are not working full-time. Other experts say the drop-out rate isn't climbing but is merely more visible now that so many women are in such high positions.

In 1994, around 9.3 million children younger than 15 had stay-at-home married mothers and working fathers, according to "Children's Living Arrangements and Characteristics: March 2002. By 2002, the number of these children rose to over 11 million.

If we are honest with ourselves, most of us do not even care for the jobs we are in. A recent poll showed that 90% of working women do not even care for their jobs. Believe it or not, 50% of babies are currently in childcare. Now isn't that a situation? Seventy-five percent of women with children over the age of 6 years old have a job away from the home. Come on now...75%! We place our family responsibilities on hold, we take our child/children to childcare, we complain about our positions on the job, and we rush home to enjoy maybe 3 hours with our family before preparing for the next cycle. Tell me, what is wrong with this picture? The enemy Satan just sits back and looks at us in the world of hustle and bustle, while our children suffer. Satan desires to sift each and every one of us.

Luke 22:31 "And the Lord said, "Simon, Simon! Indeed, Satan has asked for you, that he may sift you as wheat.

There are children letting themselves into empty homes after school unattended. They are referred to as latchkey kids. Over 59% of teens come home to an empty home. Some parents feel teens will be okay home alone. Trusting a 7-year old home alone maybe a lot better than trusting a 15 or 16-year old.

Proverbs 29:15 the rod and rebuke give wisdom, but a child left to himself brings shame to his mother.

That is where the enemy comes in and infiltrates our children's minds with thoughts that do not line up with the Word of God. Too much empty space gives the enemy too much lead in our children's lives. Now I realize everyone may not be financially able to quit her job on the spot, but use wisdom, seek God in ALL your decisions.

Matthew 6:33 but seek first the kingdom of God and His righteousness, and all these things shall be added to you.

You want to know what these are. They are <u>prosperity</u>, <u>healing</u>, <u>deliverance</u>, <u>and breakthroughs.</u>

If you want to get a great overview of what you spend and miss out on when two parents are working, take a look at your tax bracket, car insurance, car repairs, lunch, cleaners, gas, etc., and calculate how much you actually save. You would be surprised to find most people lose money. One woman shared that between her expense and actual salary, she balanced out to $39 a week. Visit www.homebodies.org and search for "Dollars and Sense". You will find financial resources that can help you achieve many things with your money!

As far the job of wife and mother, there is not enough money in the world that can pay her what the job is actually worth. There are some marriages that unfortunately have three jobs between two people. Now that is not of GOD. How are we to instill values, goals, and morality in our children if we are never available?

How in the world, can we raise a family if over 50% of our time is away from the home at some type of job? We know God is smarter than that. What would our purpose be on this earth? Now if you are blessed enough to be ahead with all of your expenses, consider your child--Is he or she worth it? Children are a privilege, not a chore! Children are our gifts from God, and they should benefit from a good Godly home. The money, promotions, job opportunities, degrees, awards are a matter of choice, our children are priceless. Nothing is wrong with wanting any of these things, but not at the expense of our children. Now if you've got it together and have struck a great balance between your job and your family. Great! Share your testimonies with others and maybe it will bless their households.

A lot of people feel a woman whose job is in the home does essentially nothing. Well, I tell you what, let the dishes go undone, ignore the laundry, don't do the cooking, or attend to the children's welfare and we will quickly see how important her job is. The home is a <u>JOB</u>, and it has its rewards.

I read a study done by Edelman Financial services, and found out the Mom at home is worth big bucks. Based on salary data from the U.S. Bureau of Labor statistics, trade groups, human resources, and staffing firms, it compiled the median annual salary for the typical Mom at home performing the services of: raising children, cooking, housecleaning, pet care, dispensing medicine, attending meetings, providing transportation, managing finances, assisting homework, maintaining family schedule, being on call 24/7, resolving problems. The work fell into over 15 key occupations. Edelman estimated that a mother's worth is about $508,700 per year – more than $42,000 a month. Wow!

In the early 1980's, people began to explore new options for living and working. There are many opportunities for women to work in their home while enjoying quality family time. Yes, legitimate ones. I have been blessed to work with some. I list quite a few later in this book. Not only women, but men are tired of the commute, the office politics, and the dead-end jobs. We are tired of squeezing in "quality time" between the late news, the laundry, and the children's bedtime stories. No wonder the divorce rate and stress rates are so high! Come on now!

Working at home is not new; it existed in the Middle Ages and during the Renaissance. According to one survey, about 40% of the total work force is either work-at-home, or self-employed. This is projected to rise about 20% each year.

Is working at home for everyone? Definitely not! Not everyone is able to handle being socially isolated. Not everyone is organized enough. Only you know what you are capable of doing.

You definitely have to be motivated and serious about this for it to work. If you are serious about working at home, you will probably find a way to make it work for you. We will look at part-time jobs you can take while your children are at school. If you have a great desire of certain goals you want to achieve, take a full-time job,--for a short time. But remember your children. I worked outside of the home for a period of time while working on this book. I truly know what my hearts desire is, and it is to totally be back in my home full-time. Through prayer and perseverance, I believe I will achieve my goal.

Often I come in contact with women that have the same values and goals that I have for my family. They realize the importance of being in the home, and raising their children. Some of these ladies have even given up their careers in order to be home with their children. One important thing about these ladies is, they are not letting the comments of others influence them. The decision they made to give up their careers to spend better quality time with their children was final. It's not just mothers of babies who are stepping out of the work force; it's mothers of older children. Mothers are realizing older children need just as much attention as babies. Don't let the world's influence take your visions in your heart.

You have to be determined - you will NOT be moved. This is happening all around the world. Women are coming back into their homes to uphold their families, and give their children values to live with forever. Pray and ask God, "What will you have me do for my family?" As you do this, your desires will become more visible to you. We all have gifts within us that could bring us great blessings. These gifts can result in our becoming quite prosperous. One thing to remember--when these gifts and talents bring us great blessings, we must not forget God. We must continue to be a light not only to our family but to this world. That is why I felt so compelled to share the work-at-home mom (WAHM) websites in this book. I feel my connection with them can open doors to you in your home that you never dreamed possible.

Chapter Six

Telecommuting, Telework Opportunities & Hottest scams revealed!

There are many benefits to working in the home, but the most important that come to my mind are:

- Time with the family. This is one of the greatest benefits.
- Second, is the flexible schedule. You save on sick time, can always take a vacation (if you have things in balance), and you have an open schedule for things that may come up.
- Third is convenience. You couldn't find a better place to work.
- Fourth, reduced costs. You eliminate lunches out, clothing, gas, parking and traffic.
- Fifth, fewer workplace distractions. You get more hours actually on the clock.
- Sixth, the potential to achieve a great income.
- Seventh, a healthier body, spirit and mind!

There are many people changing work schedules, for the simple fact they are tired of the heavy toll that the commuting is taking on their lives. Workplace and commuting stress can result in high-blood pressure, chronic headaches, back pain, alcoholism, drug abuse and disease.

Some companies now offer a 10 day work week, 7 days on 4 days off, many are even offering a telecommute schedule. Nearly eight million employees now work at home during normal business hours, according to Link Resources. This fastest-growing part of the work-from-home population is made up of salaried workers, better known as "telecommuters" or "teleworkers". This not only saves on the wear and tear on the employees, it also saves expense for the employers. Founded in 1993, the International Telework Association and Council (ITAC) is a non-profit organization dedicated to advancing the growth and success of work independent of location. ITAC sponsor Telework American holds events, distributes publications and assists businesses and the public in recognizing the advantages of working remotely. According to a series of annual reports sponsored by AT&T and managed by the International Telework Association and Council, there are approximately 28 million Americans who are teleworkers, working at home, at a telework center or satellite office; working on the road, or some combination of these.

Those who work at home reported the most substantial increase in productivity and quality since beginning work at home. Home-based workers distinguish themselves by reporting the highest job satisfaction and organization commitment and strong desire to continue working there.

Phil Montero is a virtual, mobile and home office expert who helps organizations and individuals find a more flexible way to work so they can benefit from a more balanced personal and professional life. As a speaker, coach, consultant and author, Phil uses his wealth of experience to help people learn to work more effectively from a home office, the road . . . or anywhere! Phil is the founder of YouCanWorkFromAnywhere.com providing advice, strategies, ideas and tips to help improve the productivity of telecommuters, mobile workers, entrepreneurs and home based workers. He also publishes "The Anywhere Office", a bi-weekly ezine for mobile, virtual and home office workers. Phil has allowed me to share some answers to questions that he has received during his worldwide travels. I felt this would provide a better view for those who may not be familiar with the world of telecommuting.

Here are some of the most commonly asked questions about telecommuting and mobile work:

1. How can I tell if someone who's telecommuting is working when they are outside of the office?

Managers need to be trained to focus on results rather than hours spent in the office. Completed work and progress reports will determine if goals and objectives are being met.

2. Does communication and social interaction break down causing isolation and difficulty between teleworkers and non-teleworkers

There are numerous techniques and technologies that can be taught to managers for the prevention of any breakdown in communication and social interaction. Phil teaches you proven strategies to have everyone feeling "connected" and part of the team.

3. If we implement a telecommuting program will it keep people from attending meetings?

Actually, most companies find meetings become shorter, more focused and more productive. The improved communication skills that develop as a result of telecommuting lead to workgroups being more informed and will more readily share their ideas and opinions. Phil shows you some great, affordable technology designed to help remote employees and virtual teams be more productive.

4. Are on-site employees more productive than telecommuters?

In most cases, companies have found that fewer office distractions and ownership of your own schedule create a more productive employee.

5. Who in my organization needs training to make my telecommuting initiative a success?

Organizations that have the most effective telework programs have found that educating their managers, executives, HR and IT professionals has helped them avoid costly mistakes and better prepare them to manage the challenges involved with this new way to work.

Some other teleworking opportunities to look into are:

www.clicknwork.com   This is an elite team of information specialists, business researchers and web searchers that get paid cash. This is a scam-free telework site. It is hard to qualify, but if you do you can join their virtual teams and work from anywhere in the world.

http://typist.youdictate.com/
CyberSecretaries is currently hiring legal and general typists and word processors throughout the United States and Canada to work as independent contractors from their own homes via the Internet. CyberSecretaries offers to its client base a professional product turned around in a fraction of the time of a traditional in house staff. We contract with independent legal and general transcriptionists to complete this work from their home using our software as a "key" to access the available work.

www.contractedwork.com   On this site you will be able to post your projects and receive bids from professional contractors. Freelance service providers bid on your project.

www.outsource2000.com   If you desire to work from home for a top company hiring home-based workers or in a proven business of your own, they have one of the internet's largest interactive home-based work centers.

www.hiringedge.com   Great Jobs for great people. Representing an exciting, fast paced company looking for qualified, dependable employees to fill openings for both part-time and full-time positions. This site offers you the easiest way possible to view job openings and to complete the on-line screening process.

www.liveops.com   Provides cost effective call center solutions to businesses through a completely web-enabled inbound teleservices network that operates 24 hours a day, 365 days a year.

Now let's talk about the reality and possibility of being scammed. I spent many years searching for a legitimate job and I must say I was only scammed one time. And that was totally my fault because I didn't do my homework on that company.

Here are some of the most notorious work-at-home scams I found:

Compiler or Typist Ads. The ad tells you they are accepting applications for their home data entry positions. They tell you the work is simple and can be done full or part time. The average pay is about $255 per week. As this typist you will type or write names and addresses on to a data entry form, and you will be paid, about fifty cent per name/address. What happens is these names are sold to advertisers. Usually a $10-50 application fee is involved.

Envelope-Stuffing. I use to think this was a great way to go. I was so desperate I thought everything sounded legitimate. These people usually advertise that for a "small" fee they show you how to earn money-stuffing envelopes at home. What ends up happening, for your fee, is you will more than likely get a letter telling you to place the same ads. The only way you will make money from this is if people respond to your Work-At-Home ad.

Mystery Shopping: Most ads ask for application fees from $29.95 – 49.95. This fee supplies you with a list of places and companies that hire mystery shoppers. Some scams require you to buy merchandise for a particular web site and tell you the charges will be refunded to you. I have worked with several companies as a mystery shopper. I have had great success with them. I have never paid a fee and I usually found the ads in my local newspapers. I also surfed the net and found legitimate companies. Don't go to one that asks for an application fee.

Assembly Work. These companies often require you to invest many dollars in equipment or supplies. Now I actually worked for one company cleaning lamb hair or some kind of hair for different dolls they made. This definitely wasn't for me. I was able to get my deposit back with no problem. But this is rare. On this deal, you will ultimately spend countless hours trying to produce a company product according to their standards. But after you purchase the supplies or equipment to make baby shoes, bibs, barrettes or even aprons, many companies refuse to pay for their work because it didn't meet their requirements. Most of the time, no work is ever up to their requirements.

Type from Home or Home Typing: The company tells you they provide clerical work to firms that don't have administrative staff or can't handle the workload. They usually charge an application fee from $25.00 - $200. Some require you to purchase software. Real clerical jobs do not charge fees. They even provide the software for you. If a fee is required for legitimate reasons, the company should accept major credit cards. If they ask for cash or money orders only…..DON'T DO IT!

A List of Companies looking for Home workers: In this scam you will more than likely pay a small fee for a list of companies looking for home workers just like you. The problem with this is the list is more than likely a generic listing of companies that do not take home workers. Some may have accepted home workers a long time ago.

Surveys for Cash: This also asks for a sign up fee. If you do sign up and join, you will more than likely be given a list of websites you could find on your own. I have signed up with a few sites and have paid NO fees. Here are a few for your reference.

www.acop.com
www.surveysavvy.com
www.epinions.com
www.consumerviews.com

Multi-Level Marketing. Although this is a direct sales system and usually a well-established legitimate business, it can also resemble illegitimate pyramid schemes. An obvious difference is that the emphasis is on recruiting others to join the program, not on selling the product. One thing about this system, when the system collapses, only a few people at the top have made money. Those at the bottom lose their investment.

Processing Medical Insurance Claims. The shark of this scheme attracts you by advertising on television, newspapers, trade shows and convention centers. You may be encouraged to buy software that costs thousands of dollars. You are told your work will be coordinated through insurance companies and/or doctor offices in your local area. Of course you will be pressured to make a decision immediately. If this is the case, definitely avoid it!
Some signs of a Work-at-Home Scammer are:

- They never offer you a regular salaried employment
- They promise you a big profit with part-time hours. You know the old saying: if it sounds too good to be true, it more than likely is not.
- They use personal testimonies, but don't identify the person you can contact.
- They require money for instructions or merchandise before they tell how the job works.
- Last, but not least they take your money and give you nothing in return.

The one deal I was taken for was Creative Tech of America. They promised me typing orders, processing paperwork, etc. They emailed back and forth and answered my questions promptly, provided a couple so-called references to verify the company. How bogus that was. Foolish me, I didn't check it out through the BBB (Better Business Bureau), and sent a fee of $68. They even had the nerve to send me a blank disc that was supposed to have work loaded on it. Of course, after they received my money my emails were never answered. It was like they just puffed into mid-air. I felt so foolish. I knew better. Of course I reported them to the BBB, and found there were numerous complaints.

Before dealing with any company, make sure you contact the www.bbb.org to verify if it is legitimate. Exercise caution! Legitimate work-at-home program sponsors should tell you in writing and for no charge what's involved. Make sure you document every phone call, emails, and all paperwork dealing with the company.

If you have spent money and time in a program and believe it is not legitimate, contact the company for a refund. If you can't resolve at this level contact the following agencies in the area the company is in.

- Your State Attorney's General Office
- Your State Consumer Protection Office
- The Better Business Bureau
- Your Postmaster

Also contact:
- www.scambusters.com
- www.directfraud.com

Chapter Seven

Great Legitimate Work at Home & Home schooling Resources!

The resources provided here are websites owned by work-at-home mothers. I receive newsletters and e-zines that are loaded with information on how to work and homeschool successfully in your home. I have found jobs myself through some of these websites. These women are sharing their information to help other women fulfill their dreams. They never gave up their desire or dream to be back in their home for their family. They persistently pursued what was in their heart.

Feel free to e-mail any of these addresses listed and I encourage you to sign up for the free newsletters. You will gain so much knowledge from them. Some of the sites have a nominal membership fee and I encourage you to take advantage of them.

The home school websites share so much vital information as well. The hearts and commitment these families share in home schooling their children is to be admired. For those that may have interest in home schooling and just didn't know where to start, here's your opportunity.

www.cwahm.com
CWAHM.com The online magazine for Christian Work at Home Moms. Here you'll find resources to uplift you, encourage you, and help you find a great work at home job.

www.hbwm.com
Home Based Working Mom is "the" place for home-based working moms. You can subscribe for FREE by visiting: www.hbwm.com/enews.htm. Their Monday edition focuses on Home-Based Success and the Friday Edition focuses on Family Success. And both are FREE! **HBWM** is an advocate of home business and home employment to allow parents to spend more time with their children.

www.homebodies.org
Homebodies include financial, emotional, and career-planning advice for at-home parents and working parents considering the at-home lifestyle. Whether you're aiming at becoming a full-fledged stay-at-home parent, or would just like some hints for cutting back on work while increasing time on the home front, **Homebodies** is the spot for you.

www.bizymoms.com
Bizymoms is the ultimate work at home & stay at home mom's resource site. This work from home site is building a community of moms, grandmas and dads who want to work from home or are already working from home. **Bizymoms** also offer a free newsletter with much valuable information.

www.christian-mommies.com
If you are a Christian mom looking for parenting information, support & friendship, this is the right place for you!

www.wholeheart.org
Strengthening your family to follow God wholeheartedly. **Whole Heart** will do all they can to encourage you and to equip you so you can build the kind of biblical home and godly heritage that God has put on your heart.

www.webservicenetwork.com
Web Service Network is a network of web service professionals. If you have ever dreamed of owning your own online business, now is the time! They offer resources, consultation, design & consultation, design & programming services, marketing & more!

www.familiesathome.net
Families at Home is a full resource center aiming to please the moms that desire to work at home. The resources here are sure to assist you in your quest for at-home-work.

www.motherdreams.com
MotherDreams is dedicated to helping moms make money at home online while caring for their families. Featuring work at home jobs, telecommuting, business opportunities, marketing tips, career information and other money making opportunities allowing you to work from home.

www.americanhomeschoolassociation.org
The American Homeschool Association (AHA) is a free service, non-membership organization which works to help homeschooling families and those seeking to learn more about homeschooling.

www.shesathome.com
SHE's at Home is not your ordinary WAH resource. They actually care about each visitor that enters our site. They want to build a relationship with you and make working at home as easy and stress free as possible. They offer you an easy, clutter free site to navigate and locate what you need quickly. As a stay at home executive, you have enough to worry about. Finding a respectable work at home resource should not be one of the worries.

www.homeschoolchristian.com
Your source for information and support for Christian homeschoolers. This is an unapologetically Christian Web site to aid Christian families in giving their children a superior home education. All respectful folks are welcome.

www.mommytoo.com
The first full web magazine especially created for mothers of color like you. **Mommy Too!** Magazine was designed exclusively to strengthen and encourage mothers of color to be well and live well, while also empowering women of color to view themselves as women *as well as* mothers. We promote and embrace a new motherhood ideal; one in

which you're not just wife, sister, employee, daughter, friend and companion, but
mommy too!

www.womans-net
Woman-Net is an Online Networking Community for Women. They can help you reach your goals by helping you network with other women through our global community.

www.amomslove.com
A Mom's Love is a monthly online magazine full of insightful articles. They support all moms – with pages for stay at home, work at home, single and working moms!

www.youdictate.com
Cyber Secretaries is an Internet-based transcription service available around the clock and around the world, from any telephone. Your dictation is transcribed, proofread and sent back (via email) to your computer - often in less time than an on-site staff is able to provide.

www.homeschoolcentral.com
All the resources you need! A guide to homeschool resources and services that will help you successfully homeschool your children.

www.dotcommommies.com
DotCommommies specializes in working at home and making money online for a better life. Many work at home jobs, telecommuting, business opportunities, marketing surveys, and other moneymaking opportunities are found.

www.wahmiam.com
WAHM I am website celebrates the work-at-home-mom. or "WAHM". Through educating, promoting, servicing, supporting and rewarding. There will be great advertising specials periodically also, so check back for those.

www.achristianconnection.com
A Christian Connection Newsletter is designed to get you the information, tools, and education you need in order to: Be home with your family – Give your children the advantage in business education and entrepreneurial skills – Homeschool your children – Get out of debt or take control of your finances – Encouragement in all areas of life – Tools and education for business – Inform you of Christian businesses, Christian conferences, seminars and retreats.

www.RaisingOurKids.com
Raising Our Kids is where you can find advice and friendship to guide and support you through the trials and tribulations of raising children. This site offers a large variety of resource including parenting articles, advice, free coloring pages, links to useful websites, message boards, and just about anything else a parent or grandparent could want.

www.homewiththekids.com
A resource for parents who want to stay home with their kids, whether by saving enough money to get by on one income or by finding a legitimate work at home job or home business opportunity.

www.mommerce.com
Mommerce exist because we love babies. Their goal is to be the website of choice for parents-to-be and those who want to buy them unique gifts. Please browse through their on-line catalog; they're sure you'll find what you need (or at least something that you want).

www.easyhomeschooling.net
FREE homeschooling resources! Easy Homeschooling books! Yes, homeschooling can be FREE! **Easy Homeschooling** 5-Star books are unique in offering concise and highly usable homeschooling information - and LOTS of it! The **Easy Homeschooling** site offers FREE resources!

www.mypreciouskid.com
MyPreciousKid emphasizes that you must protect your kids and give them an extra measure of security with their Kid's ID Card Kits or Children's ID/Fingerprint/DNA Kits! Children's Safety Products to protect your children! Kid Safety is their priority! The sales rep program was born when others asked how they could share the products in their communities too! Kay loves helping other moms have a successful work at home business too!

www.amomsjoy.com
A Moms Joy brings moms together to learn, laugh and enjoy! Features at home resources, themed party ideas, message boards and much more.

www.christianfamilytreasures.com
Christian Family Treasures is a site designed for women who are interested in Christian values, parenting, recipes, home life, a home-based business opportunity, and they have many more Christian family resources coming soon!

www.contemporarymoms.com
A place where today's moms share the many facets of motherhood.

www.momsplaza.com
The online plaza for all your shopping needs. If you're looking for that special something or are just in the mood to shop, you've come to the right place. The **Moms Plaza** is an Online store for all your shopping needs. These items are sold by today's moms. Moms who know and understand what you need and want.

www.thehomeschoolmom.com
Homeschool or home school: no matter how you spell it, homeschooling is a viable option for more families every year. **TheHomeSchoolMom** guides you through the free homeschooling resources available online, making the most of your budget and your planning time.

www.usawahm.com
Usawahm is helping you succeed in your business.

www.webmomz.com
Webmomz is empowering moms to start a home business and make money working from home!

www.christianwahmnetwork.com
Christian WAHM Network is a place for Christian home-based business owners to network, find business resources, share ideas, and help encourage and promote one another.

www.mommytips.com
Mommytips is your complete resource for all things related to home and parenting. Expert information, fun contests, tons of freebies, informative articles, safety recalls, shopping and so much more

www.mompack.com
Mompack is a group of moms in business who work together to build their businesses.

www.mommyco.com
MommyCo is an association of offline business groups and an online community of parents who work at home or who want to work at home. Andrea King-Dalton is the Owner/Director of **MommyCo™**. In her own quest to stay at home with her three children she was faced with many challenges and accepted her share of defeats. She realizes how difficult it is to balance work with family. But it can be done! If you've ever felt isolated or frustrated in your work efforts, you've come to the right place. **MommyCo™** is devoted to helping working mothers keep their family a priority; with online *and* offline support and resources. By joining **MommyCo** you can talk to other working moms, find an offline **MommyCo** home business group in your area, or learn how to find a telecommuting job so you can stay home with your kids while working.

www.busymomsrecipes.com
Busy Moms Recipes™ is a Christian-based site that features a sampling of the quick and easy-to-prepare recipes and inspirational

messages that are emailed to members in our monthly newsletter. Along with the recipes, they also feature the "best of the web" selections, including freebies, cooking tips, contests, and more. They invite you to browse around their site and look at their recipes, inspirations and freebies, using the links below. Then, come back "home" to sign up to join our FREE mailing list.

www.dabblingmum.com
The Dabbling Mum Online magazine for BUSY parents with centers for home business, writing, parenting, parties and a free monthly contest.

www.christian-mommies.com
Christian Mommies is a site for moms to find the every day parenting tips they are searching for *and* to grab a moment for themselves.

www.homeschoolingadventures.com
All your homeschooling needs in one spot. FREE worksheets, lesson plans, activities, laws. Tons of links to everything educational.

www.homefireshearth.com
Homesfireshearth is a family-friendly newsletter for Christian Homemakers, including those working outside the home. To support each individual as they put on the armor of God, Biblically and spiritually, as brothers and sisters in Christ, so we as the family of believers may go out into the world and do Gods will, and to help prepare our families for the next world with Jesus.

www.christianhomekeeper.com
Find help and encouragement for being a stay at home Mother and wife, read about godly women and their homes, find out how to have a peaceful godly home, find homeschool unit studies and more.

www.wahmliving.com
Wahm Living helps moms find their work at home niche. Try their Niche quiz. It will help point you in the right direction on

your work at home journey. Once you find out what type of home business is right for you, take a look at their Niche Categories. They have work at home opportunities advertised in each category; maybe one will fit your needs!

www.heart4home.net
Heart 4 home offers creative gifts for sharing. It is also loaded with practical and fun ideas from anything as budgeting, decorating, meal planning, organization, e-books, grocery, homemaking and much more.

www.wahmtalkradio.com
Wahm Talk Radio is an on demand Internet Radio for the Work at Home Mom! Tune in and receive a great message for your heart.

www.mompreneursonline.com
Pat Cobe and Ellen Parlapiano have over 25 years of work-from-home experience. Moms themselves, they are experts on juggling a home business and a family under the same roof. They write and lecture on work-from-home and time management topics, and consult for corporations like ATT and American Express. Their weekly "**Mompreneurs®**" advice column, message board and chats appear on iVillage.com, which is visited by 7 million women each month. Cobe and Parlapiano are also on the advisory board for Home-Based Working Moms, a national organization in Texas. Find out why and how mom-owned businesses are surviving and thriving on the Web…even though many big dot.coms are closing their doors.

www.Christian-Parent.com
Resources for the Christian family, including parenting, marriage, family traditions, holidays, book reviews, and more.

www.christianhomeschoolcommunity.com
Christian Homeschool Community is an online community of families who desire to serve the Lord. Some are in the process of homeschooling, others are grandparents and others are just considering home education as an option. They invite you to stop by! Their desire is for this site to provide encouragement and

resources for Christian families that will assist you in your service to your family at home.

www.mumshomeworks.com
Mum's Homeworks Asia is a professional on-line community of mothers or women who would like to work from home and those who are already working from home. They provide support, networking opportunities, information, email discussions on mothers or women related issues, publicity opportunities and more.

www.2work-at-home.com
2Work-At-Home com has been providing free work at home job listings, home business ideas, and many other free work at home resources since 1999.

www.wahmfest.org
WAHMfest™ believes the role of Mother is the proudest occupation in the world. However, they also understand, from experience, that moms often need something "for themselves" - and many have a desire to feel that they are contributing materially to their family's well-being. **WAHMfest**™ is dedicated to helping moms stay at home with their children and still be able to fulfill their *own* needs, as well.

www.organized-mom.com
Everyday hints and tips for getting your life and your family more organized.

www.aimingatmoms.com
Melissa wanted a website where moms and moms-to-be could get parenting tips, great shopping links, job opportunities and a feeling that they are not alone in the mom business. There's even a page for daddy's, but only if you are a Yankee Fan. GO YANKS!! This website is just her way to give back to all the moms out there working as hard as she is.

www.teleworkrecruiting.com
Telework Recruiting is your targeted source for virtual workers and employment!

www.wahm.com
Work At Home Moms is an online magazine for moms who work at home. Includes monthly features, helpful hints, stories, and links to WAHM businesses.

www.proverbs31.org
Proverbs 31 Ministries is dedicated to glorifying God by touching women's hearts to build Godly homes. Through Jesus Christ, they shed light on God's distinctive design for women and the great responsibilities we have been given. With Proverbs 31:10-31 as a guide, they encourage and equip women to practice the Seven Principles of the Proverbs 31 Woman.

www.jobsformoms.com
Jobs for Moms is an online service for moms who enjoy being with their children. Jobs for moms work at home program was featured on Lifetime TV as an online home based job database for finding scam-free work-at-home jobs.

www.budgetmom.com
If you are like most moms, you love a bargain and you love to save money where you can. **BudgetMom.com** is the perfect place for the frugal minded mom. Their site is simple and filled with the savings you want. AND you'll find discounts and specials you WON'T find anywhere else in their bonus savings area. Be sure to bookmark them to print out all the coupons you need, they have thousands available to you. They have national, local and specialty coupons along with the best freebies and offers around.

www.mymommybiz.com
My Mommy Biz is for work-at-home moms. Your complete guide for starting your very own business from ideas and business names to sales and marketing techniques.

www.momsnetwork.com
Moms Network celebrates moms at home and in business. While **Moms Network** doesn't provide jobs or employment, it offers

resources for you whether you want to work for yourself or for someone else. So, dig in, take your time, and make your decisions wisely.

www.workathomeparents.com
Work at Home Parents is a free work at home resource inspiring parents to work at home. The newsletter inspires and helps work at home parents. We feature articles to help you make money with marketing tips, inspiration quotes, time saving cooking recipes, freebies, and classifieds.

www.homeschoolbuzz.com
Homeschooling in the news!! This site is to bring you stories of homeschooling to encourage, inspire and inform.

www.homeworkingmom.com
Mother's Home Business Network is the first and largest national organization providing ideas, inspiration and support for mothers who choose to work at home. They have been helping mothers become home-working mothers since 1984.

www.4workathomemothers.com
4 Work at Home Mothers is a great site for parents! They have compiled a great source of interesting links, fascinating articles, and fun diversions for mothers who stay and work at home.

www.workaholics4hire.com
Workaholics 4 Hire – Telecommuting Jobs – Staffing solutions for the new economy! The Internet is being flooded with telecommuting jobs, but few people have the understanding of how to find them. Sylvie Charrier successfully researched this topic and **Workaholics4hire** was born in early 1997.

www.million-dollar-mama.com
Girlfriend getaways, girl's night out, women's fitness, spa pampering, articles and resources – for mothers by mothers.

www.CyberCityMommies.com
The Home Business Connection for Work at Home Moms.

www.momzone.com
Mom Zone is a member of Moms Network online community. It is one of the best new sites on the net for moms. Take advantage of their services and join in the popular Community Forums where you will meet thousands of other moms just like you.

www.homeschoolmom.com
HomeSchoolMom is a newsletter for you - the mom, teacher, wife, coach, chief operating officer (COO) of your home. **HomeSchoolMom** is a free newsletter that will bring you insights and helpful tips in many of the areas a homeschooling mom needs encouragement. The owner has an upcoming book on homeschooling young children - preschool through second grade. She's looking to include 1st year accounts of homeschool moms.

www.familyandhome.org
Family and Home is a monthly journal for parents who forgo or cut back on paid employment to engage in the challenges and joys of nurturing their children of all ages.

www.momscareer.com
Moms Career offers legitimate jobs, business opportunities and resources that allow you to work-from-home and have the life you always wanted! The site features work-at-home jobs, and local telecommuting opportunities.

www.homeschool.com
Your virtual homeschool! Homeschool.com's Top Choice. New! Ablaze Learning - Accredited, Internet Based with Live Tutors.

www.emommies.net
eMommies.net is a community developed by moms, for moms. At **eMommies.net** they are dedicated to providing ALL types of moms with excellent service and superior resources. **eMommies.net** recognizes that while every mother is unique in her goals and ideals, we all strive to be the best mommies we are capable of being.

www.SheLovesGod.com
She Loves God is a support community for Christian women. Read/submit articles, inspirational stories, & poems. A Christian support community helping you progress spiritually.

www.womenoffaith.com
Women of Faith is an interdenominational women's ministry committed to helping women of all faiths, backgrounds, age groups, and nationalities. Women of Faith was founded specifically to meet the needs of women. We are committed to helping women grow emotionally, spiritually and in relationships: whether marriages, friendships, the workplace and/or with their children.

www.marykay.com/tanyamwhite
Mary Kay offers you an opportunity where you can start living the balanced, rewarding life you want. Discover how easy it is to enjoy financial success while nurturing your faith and your family.

www.shopping4pay.com
Undercover shoppers – paid to shop, dine & more. Finally a work at home opportunity that is fun, flexible and easy!

www.4parentsnetwork.com
4 Parents Network is helping you navigate all ages & stages of parenting.

www.homeschooltoday.com
The work of **Homeschooling Today** magazine is focused and specific. Their commitment to bring the homeschool community useful information and resources is supported by a Biblical conviction that God uses families to change the world.

www.hearts-at-home.org
Hearts at Home is a ministry dedicated to professionalizing motherhood. They offer professional weekend conferences and a monthly magazine and a devotional to encourage mothers at home or those who want to be. Keynote speakers, workshops, drama and music fill the weekends with opportunities for encouragement,

personal growth, new ideas, fresh perspective and renewed vision for this important role."

www.mommysplace.net
Mommy's Place is an award-winning job site, providing some of the best resources and company leads on real home-based employment.

www.homeschoolzone.
Homeschoolzone welcome not only homeschoolers, but educators, parents and kids in public & private schools around the world--- They have many FREE newsletters & services and great ways to connect with people and more.

www.womenbygrace.com
Women By Grace is based in beautiful Gaylord, Michigan. They are in their fourth year of ministry to women and they are excited about everything God has been doing in their women, their church and through this website! Womenbygrace.com is intended to be a resource to all women.

Mark 9:23 - Jesus said to him, "If you can believe, all things are possible to him who believes".

Sometimes it may seem so easy to believe the negative. One thing I have learned is that to accomplish great dreams you must be determined to succeed! Remember if it was so easy to achieve, everyone would be doing it!

Here are a few ideas of jobs that you can do right in your home:

Arts and Crafts
Beauty Salon
Childcare Services
Cake Decorating
Candy Making
Catering Service
Cleaning Service
Elderly Care Services

Exercise for Seniors
Product Demonstrators
Flower Arrangements
Garage Sale Service
Manicure Service
Mystery Shopping
Pet Sitting
Tutorial Services
Typing Service
Wedding Consultant

Chapter Eight

The Daily Word

No matter what issues in life you face, God has provided and prepared a way of escape.

1 Corinthians 10:13 No temptation has overtaken you except such as is common to man; but God is faithful, who will not allow you to be tempted beyond what you are able, but with the temptation will also make the way of escape, that you may be able to bear it.

Scripture not only gives you encouragement, but provides the source of strength you need for your daily guidance. Look at it this way, we basically eat three daily meals to survive physically, well we also need daily meals to survive spiritually. If we take care of our spirit as much as we do our flesh, we will always be fulfilled! We must not take lightly the life we've been given.

Godliness

Favour is deceitful, and beauty is vain; but a woman that feareth the Lord, she shall be praised. **Proverbs 31:30**

Who can find a virtuous woman? For her price is far above rubies. The heart of her husband doth safely trust in her, so that he shall have no need of spoil. She will do him good and not evil all the days of her life. **Proverbs 31: 10-12**

But refuse profane and old wives' fables, and exercise thyself rather unto Godliness. **1 Timothy 4:7**

No man can serve two masters; for either he will hate the one, and love the other; or else he will hold to the one, and despise the other. Ye cannot serve God and mammon. **Matthew 6:24**

I beseech you therefore, brethren, by the mercies of God, that ye present your bodies a living sacrifice, holy, acceptable unto God, which is your reasonable service. **Romans 12:1**

Love

That they may teach the young women to be sober, to love their husbands, to love their children. **Titus 2:4**

I rejoiced greatly that I found of thy children walking in truth, as we have received a commandment from the Father. And now I beseech thee, lady, not as though I wrote a new commandment unto thee, but that which we had from the beginning, that we love one another. **2 John 1: 4-5**

I love them that love me; and those that seek me early shall find me. **Proverbs 3:17-19**

But God commendeth his love toward us, in that, while we were yet sinners, Christ died for us. **Romans 5:8**

Sacrifice

Wives, submit yourselves unto your own husbands, as it is fit in the Lord. **Colossians 3:18**

Likewise, ye wives, be in subjection to your own husbands; that, if any obey not the word, they also may without the word be won by the conversation of the wives. **1 Peter 3:1**

Let us hold fast the profession of our faith without wavering: (for he is faithful that promised). **Hebrews 10:23**

Wait on the Lord; be of good courage, and he shall strengthen thine heart: wait, I say, on the Lord. **Psalm 27:14**

Compassion

It is the Lord's mercies that we are not consumed, because his compassions fail not. They are new every morning; great is thy faithfulness. The Lord is my portion, saith my soul; therefore will I hope in him. **Lamentations 3: 22-24**

Fruitfulness

And she spake out with a loud voice, and said, Blessed art thou among women, and blessed is the fruit of thy womb. **Luke 1:42**

And she called his name Joseph; and said, The Lord shall add to me another son. **Genesis 30:24**

Thy wife shall be as a fruitful vine by the sides of thine house: thy children like olive plants round about thy table. **Psalm 128:3**

Grace

And his mercy is on them that fear him from generation to generation. **Luke 1:50**

And when the Lord saw her, he had compassion on her, and said unto her Weep not. **Luke 7:13**

And he said unto me, My grace is sufficient for thee: for my strength is made perfect in weakness. Most gladly therefore will I rather glory in my infirmities, that the power of Christ may rest upon me. **II Corinthians 12:9**

Guidance

For this God is our God forever and ever; he will be our guide even unto death. **Psalm 48:14**

For the Holy Ghost shall teach you in the same hour what ye ought to say. **Luke 12:12**

Thy word is a lamp unto my feet, and a light unto my path. **Psalm 119:105**

The steps of a good man are ordered by the Lord: and he delighteth in his way. **Psalm 37:23**

Honor

A gracious woman retaineth honour; and strong men retain riches. **Proverbs 11:16**

Honour thy father and thy mother, that thy days may be long upon the land which the Lord thy God giveth thee. **Exodus 20:12**

All Scripture is given by inspiration of God, and is profitable for doctrine, for reproof, for correction, for instruction in righteousness. **II Timothy 3:16**

Joy

He maketh the barren woman to keep house, and to be a joyful mother of children. Praise ye the Lord. **Psalm 113:9**

This is the day which the Lord hath made; we will rejoice and be glad in it. **Psalm 118:24**

Protection

But the Lord is faithful, who shall stablish you, and keep you from evil. **2 Thessalonians 3:3**

For he shall give His angels charge over you, to keep you in all your ways. **Psalm 91:11**

With long life I will satisfy him, And show him my salvation. **Psalm 91:16**

Behold, I give you the authority to trample on serpents and scorpions, and over all power of the enemy, and nothing shall by any means harm you. **Luke 10:19**

Trust

Trust in the Lord, and do good; so shalt thou dwell in the land, and verily thou shalt be fed. Delight thyself also in the Lord; and he shall give thee the desires of thy heart. **Psalm 37:3-4**

Cast thy burden upon the Lord, and he shall sustain thee: he shall never suffer the righteous to be moved. **Psalm 55:22**

My help cometh from the Lord, which made heaven and earth. He will not suffer thy foot to be moved: he that keepeth thee will not slumber. **Psalm 121: 2-3**

Jesus saith unto him, I am the way, the truth, and the life: no man cometh unto the Father, but by me. **John 14:6**

Understanding

Come unto me, all ye that labour and are heavy laden, and I will give you rest. Take my yoke upon you, and learn of me; for I am meek and lowly in heart: and ye shall find rest unto your souls. For my yoke is easy, and my burden is light. **Matthew 11: 28-30**

Children

Lo, children are a heritage of the Lord: ad the fruit of the womb is his reward. **Psalm 127:3**

And all thy children shall be taught of the lord; and great shall be the peace of thy children. **Isaiah 54:13**

Faith

Therefore being justified by faith, we have peace with God through our Lord Jesus Christ: By whom also we have access by faith into this grace wherein we stand, and rejoice in hope of the glory of God. **Romans 5: 1-2**

For with God nothing shall be impossible. **Luke 1:37**

But ye, beloved, building up yourselves on your most holy faith, praying in the Holy Ghost. Keep yourselves in the love of God, looking for the mercy of our Lord Jesus Christ unto eternal life. **Jude 1: 20-21**

Enemies

Submit yourselves therefore to God. Resist the devil, and he will flee from you. Draw nigh to God, and he will draw nigh to you, cleanse your hand, ye sinners; purify your hearts, ye double minded. **James 4: 7-8**

The Lord shall preserve thee from all evil: he shall preserve thy soul. The Lord shall preserve thy going out and thy coming in from this time forth, and even for evermore. **Psalm 121: 7-8**

Be ye angry, and sin not: let not the sun go down upon your anger: Neither give place to the devil. **Ephesians 4: 26-27**

And be not conformed to this world; but be ye transformed by the renewing of your mind, that ye may prove what is that good, and acceptable, and perfect, will of God. **Romans 12:2**

For the weapons of our warfare are not carnal, but mighty through God to the pulling down of strongholds. **2 Corinthians 10:4**

Trials

I can do all things through Christ which strengtheneth me. **Philippians 4:13**

Cast thy burden upon the Lord, and he shall sustain thee: he shall never suffer the righteous to be moved. **Psalm 55:22**

He that covereth his sins shall not prosper: but whoso confesseth and forsaketh them shall have mercy. **Proverbs 28:13**

Submit yourselves therefore to God. Resist the devil, and he will flee from you. **James 4:7**

Stress

If the Son therefore shall make you free, ye shall be free indeed. **John 8:36**

Peace I leave with you, my peace I give unto you; not as the world giveth, give I unto you. Let not your heart be troubled, neither let it be afraid. **John 14: 27**

For God hath not given us the spirit of fear; but of power, and of love, and of a sound mind. Who hath saved us, and called us with an holy calling, not according to our works, but according to his own purpose and grace, which was given us in Christ Jesus before the world began. **2 Timothy 1: 7, 9**

Casting all your care upon him; for he careth for you. **I Peter 5:7**

Let not your heart be troubled; ye believe in God, believe also in me. **John 14:1**

Thou wilt keep him in perfect peace, whose mind is stayed on thee: because he trusteth in thee. **Isaiah 26:3**

Prayer

Again I say unto you that if two of you shall agree on earth as touching anything that they shall ask, it shall be done for them of my Father which is in heaven. **Matthew 18:19**

Be careful for nothing: but in everything by prayer and supplication with thanksgiving let your requests be made known unto God. **Philippians 4:6**

Let us therefore come boldly unto the throne of grace, that we may obtain mercy, and find grace to help in time of need. **Hebrews 4:16**

But without faith it is impossible to please him: for he that cometh to God must believe that he is, and he is a rewarder of them that diligently seek him. **Hebrews 11:6**

And all things, whatsoever ye shall ask in prayer, believing, ye shall receive. **Matthew 21:22**

If ye abide in me, and my words abide in you, ye shall ask what ye will, and it shall be done unto you. **John 15:7**

Protection

I am the good shepherd: the good shepherd giveth his life for his sheep. **John 10:11**

The angel of the Lord encampeth round about them that fear him, and delivereth them. **Psalm 34:7**

But whose hearkeneth unto me shall dwell safely, and shall be quiet from fear of evil. **Proverbs 1:33**

Suffering

We are troubled on every side, yet not distressed; we are perplexed, but not in despair; Persecuted, but not forsaken; cast down, but not destroyed; Always bearing about in the body the dying of the Lord Jesus, that the life also of Jesus might be made manifest in our body. **2 Corinthians 4: 8-10**

For our light affliction, which is but for a moment, worketh for us a far more exceeding; and eternal weight of glory; While we look not at the things which are seen, but at the things which are not seen: for the things which are seen are temporal; but the things which are not seen are eternal. **2 Corinthians 4: 17-18**

Thou therefore endure hardness, as a good soldier of Jesus Christ. **2 Timothy 2:3**

For even hereunto were ye called: because Christ also suffered for us, leaving us an example, that ye should follow his steps. **1 Peter 2:21**

Victory

Have not I commanded thee? Be strong and of a good courage; be not afraid, neither be thou dismayed: for the Lord thy God is with the withersoever thou goest. **Joshua 1:9**

This is the day which the Lord hath made: we will rejoice and be glad in it. Save now, I beseech thee, O Lord: O Lord, I beseech thee, send now prosperity. **Psalm 118: 24-25**

Notwithstanding ye have well done, that ye did communicate with my affliction. **Philippians 4: 12-14**

And ye shall eat in plenty, and be satisfied, and praise the name of the Lord your God, that hath dealt wondrously with you: and my people shall never be ashamed. **Joel 2:26**

Addiction

Stand fast therefore in the liberty wherewith Christ hath made us free, and be not entangled again with the yoke bondage. **Galatians 5:1**

Wine is a mocker, strong drink is raging : and whosoever is deceived thereby is not wise. **Proverbs 20:1**

Bitterness

Let all bitterness, and wrath, and anger, and clamour, and evil speaking, be put away from you, with all malice. **Ephesians 4:31**

Looking diligently lest any man fail of the grace of God; lest any root of bitterness springing up trouble you and thereby many be defiled. **Hebrews 12:15**

But if you have bitter envying and strife in your hearts, glory not, and lie not against the truth. This wisdom descendeth not from above, but is earthly, sensual, devilish. **James 3; 14-15**

Forbearing one another, and forgiving one another, if any man have a quarrel against any: even as Christ forgave you, so also do ye. **Colossians 3:13**

Confusion

For my thoughts are not your thoughts, neither are your ways my ways, saith the Lord. For as the heavens are higher than the earth, so are my ways higher than your ways, and my thoughts than your thoughts. **Isaiah 55:8-9**

For God is not the author of confusion, but of peace, as in all churches of the saints. 1 **Corinthians 14:33**

Grief

He will swallow up death in victory; and the Lord God will wipe away tears from off all faces; and the rebuke of his people shall he take away from off all the earth: for the Lord hath spoken it. **Isaiah 25:8**

For the Lord hath comforted his people, and will have mercy upon his afflicted. **Isaiah 49:13b**

Blessed are they that mourn: for they shall be comforted. **Matthew 5:4**

Depression

Finally, brethen, whatsoever things are true, whatsoever things are honest, whatsoever things are just, whatsoever things are pure, whatsoever things are lovely, whatsoever things are of good report; if there be any virture, and if there be any praise, think on these things. **Philippians 4:8**

I will not leave you comfortless: I will come to you. **John 14:18**

He healeth the broken in heart, and bindeth up their wounds. **Psalm 147:3**

Be strong and of good courage, fear not, nor be afraid of them: for the Lord thy God, he it is that doth go with thee: he will not fail thee, nor forsake thee. **Deuteronomy 31:6**

Finances

Buy my God shall supply all your need according to his riches in glory by Christ Jesus. **Philippians 4:19**

Beloved, I wish above all things that thou mayest prosper and be in health, even as thy soul prospereth. **III John 2**

The Lord is my shephed: I shall not want. **Psalm 23:1**

Give, and it shall be given unto you; good measure, pressed down, and shaken together, and running over, shall men give into your bosom. For with the same measure that ye mete withal it shall be measured to you again. **Luke 6:38**

Healing

Is any sick among you? Let him call for the elders of the church; and let them pray over him, anointing him with oil in the name of the Lord. **James 5:14**

Who forgiveth all thine iniquities: who healeth all thy diseases. **Psalm 103:3**

For I will restore health unto thee, and I will heal thee of thy wounds, saith the Lord. **Jeremiah 30:17a**

Loneliness
I will not leave you comfortless: I will come to you. **John 14:18**

He healeth the broken in heart, and bindeth up their wounds. **Psalm 147:3**

One thing I must add. If you haven't accepted Jesus Christ as your personal Savior, you can <u>TODAY!</u> I tell you it is very easy to become a believer, and walk in all of God's promises.

Roman 10:9 "that if you confess with your mouth the Lord Jesus and Believe in your heart that God has raised Him from the dead, you will be saved". John 3:16 For God so loved the world that He gave His only begotten Son, that whoever believes in Him should not perish but have everlasting life. 2 Corinthians 5:17 Therefore, if anyone is in Christ, he is a new creation; old things have passed away; behold, all things have become new.

"THE SINNER PRAYER"

Father, in the name of Jesus, I confess right now, and realize that I am a sinner. I repent of all my sins. I commit my life to you today! I change my heart, I change my mind, I change my direction, and I turn toward Jesus Christ. I confess with my mouth that Jesus died and God raised him from the dead on the third day, and I believe in my heart that Jesus is alive and operates in my life today. I thank you Lord that I am SAVED. Amen!

A Parent's Prayer

O Heavenly Father make me a better parent. Teach me to understand my children, to listen patiently to what they have to say, and to answer all their questions kindly. Keep me from interrupting them or contradicting them. Make me as courteous to them as I would have them be to me. Forbid that I should ever laugh at their mistakes, or resort to shame or ridicule them when they displease me. May I never punish them for my own selfish satisfaction or to show my power. Let me not tempt my child to lie or steal. And guide me hour by hour that I may demonstrate by all I say and do that honesty produces happiness. Reduce, I pray the meanness in me. And when I am out of sorts, help me, O Lord, to hold my tongue. May I ever be mindful that my children are children and that I should not expect of them the judgments of adults. Let me not rob them of the opportunity to wait on themselves and to make decisions. Bless me with the bigness to grant them all their reasonable requests and the courage to deny them privileges I know will do them harm. Make me fair and just and kind. And fit me, O Lord, to be loved and respected and imitated by my children.

Author Unknown

"The Woman: Who is She?"

She is a woman whom God has blessed;
she has class, she has style, she has finesse.
She is one who can comfort with just one single word;
her words will share love, peace, and patience, it's nothing unheard.
Who is this woman whom God has blessed?
She is a woman who has the heart of her husband,
and makes it through every trial, temptation and test.
She is a woman who guides her children in all perfect ways;
for she knows their life is in her hands,
for she is their example to lengthen their days.
Sometimes she feels her efforts are worthless,
they seem to go with no thanks;
but God knows her heart is pure and her rewards will be great!
Let's not take her for granted, for she feels like you do;
she would give you the clothes off her back,
just to show you she is honest and true.

"Our Children"

Our children are special
because God made them that way.
They are not our children of the future,
but they are our children of today!
They have visions, goals, and dreams they want to achieve,
so don't take them so lightly; supply them with their every need.
Can you honestly say you've done all you can do?
Don't speak much too soon because our children will speak the truth about you!
It won't be very long when they will be
our doctors, lawyers, even our President you see.
Just be sure you are doing your part to help make them succeed!

"Family and Friends"

Family and friends are very special you see; they are loved ones that they can
depend on; they will be there to help us with every need!
Sometimes they may make us discouraged, they may frustrate us at every cost; one thing I must say for sure, it's not worth the relationship lost.
Once we understand the importance of God's covenant, we would never think
of being apart; for our family and friends are simply the closest one's that can get to our heart.
Let's not take each other for granted, remember Jesus died for you too; we
should never, ever become too proud, just to say "I love you!"

Printed in the United States
35378LVS00007B/202-246